About the Author

Lizi Gambell is a home educating mum, remedial hypnotist, artist and tattooist. She lives in Kent in the UK with her husband Jim and their two sons, Rufus and Otis. They have been unschooling since 2015.

After establishing their own creative business in their early twenties, Lizi and Jim started a family. Home education first appeared on the radar after their eldest son started school, and they saw their little boy changing in ways they never imagined. Pulled to look for alternatives, they found their way to unschooling, and continued on that path to this day.

Since 2017, Lizi has worked as a Control practitioner, using hypnosis to enable clients to let go of emotional and behavioural barriers, and upgrade their confidence and self-esteem. She is also the founder of Hypnotattoo, a revolutionary process which sets positive affirmations in the skin.

To learn more about Lizi's work, visit
www.hypnotattoo.com

THE UNSCHOOLED LIFE

One Family's Home Education Adventure

LIZI GAMBELL

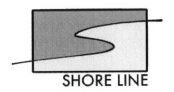

SHORE LINE

a shore line book
First published in paperback and ebook 2019

Cover art courtesy of Sam Cannon
www.samcannonart.co.uk

Shore Line is an imprint of Wide Open Sea • Art • Heritage • Press
1 (A1F153) Summerhall
Edinburgh
EH9 1PL
www.shorelinebooks.co.uk
www.wideopensea.co.uk

The ISBN for this book is 978-1-9161148-0-7
A CIP catalogue record for this book is available from the
British Library.

A child is a bell of mindfulness, reminding us how marvellous life is.

Thich Nhat Hanh

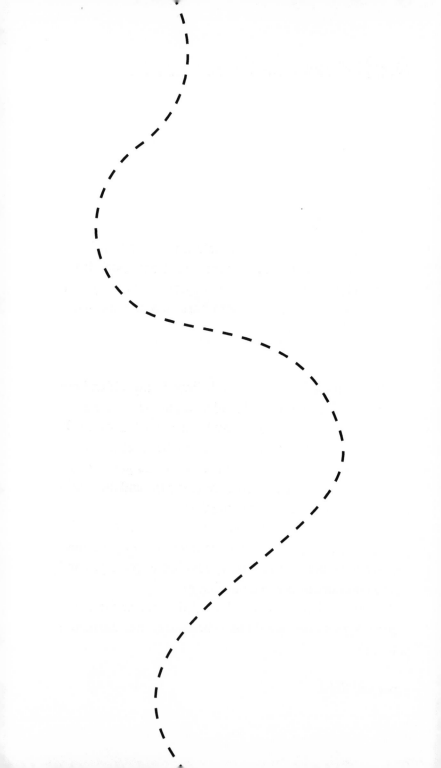

Acknowledgments

Throughout this book I have included quotes that I find inspiring and energising. Some are from established writers and thinkers, others are anonymous or apocryphal. I have tried to credit sources where they are known – please forgive any oversight.

I would like to thank...

My parents for raising me to believe in myself and my two beautiful sisters who shared a childhood with me.

My husband Jim, who always helps me to think outside the box and to question everything I believe; he is my parenting partner and my best friend. My gorgeous boys, who constantly teach me more about myself and the world than I ever knew before meeting them.

All the amazing, creative, enlightened people who have crossed my path and opened my mind. In particular, my hypnotist mentor Tim Box, who has encouraged and pushed me forwards since our first meeting.

My sister Alice, without whose dedication and creative approach, this book would have been only half the read it is today.

Love and light.

Contents

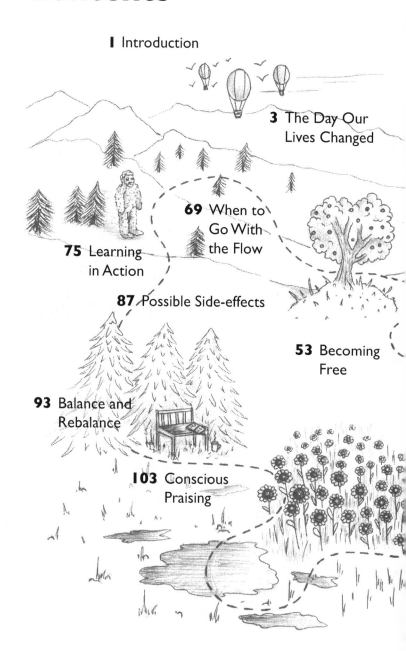

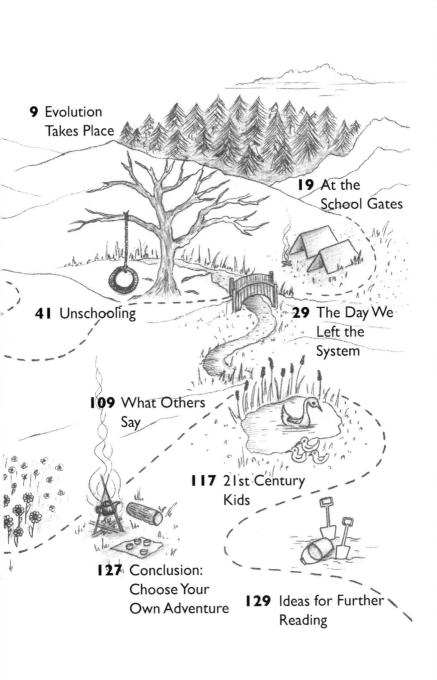

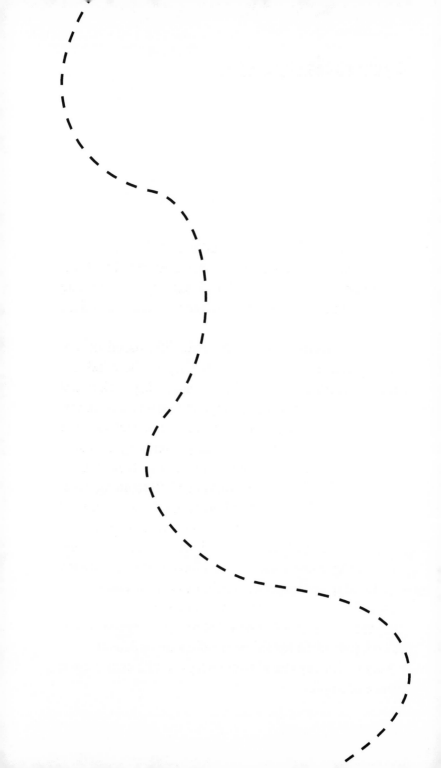

Introduction

This is the book I wish was available at the start of our adventure in home education. It is my intention that it will help others explore the wild and exciting unschooling lifestyle with emotional intelligence and a raised awareness.

I have included tips for an easier life, based on my own experiences and my understanding of the mind and emotions from being a remedial hypnotist. My wish is that you gain something positive for your own unique journey.

This book is arranged into thirteen chapters. The first part tells how our lives changed one day in 2008, and then changed and changed again as our family grew. The chapters 'Unschooling' (p.41) and 'Becoming Free' (p.53) describe how we found unschooling, and the hard but necessary process of deschooling that followed.

The second part of the book shares some of the practical suggestions and advice I have learned along the way. Read it from start to finish, or drop in and out for hints and encouragement when you need it.

At the end, you will find a list of books mentioned in the text, plus ideas for further reading and guidance.

May you always tread your own path with courage and balance of mind.

Sometimes, the smallest step in the right direction ends up being the biggest step of your life.

Naeem Calloway

Chapter 1
The Day Our Lives Changed

This is a book about home educating by a mum in the thick of it, bringing up two boys, running two businesses and trying to keep a home in order. But this story begins a long time ago. On the chilly morning of New Year's Day, 2008.

Jim, my best friend and partner of ten years, is sleeping off a New Year's Eve hangover of epic proportions. I sit in the bathroom, in shock. In my shaking hand I hold a pregnancy test. A positive pregnancy test. My brain is flipping out, throwing itself from left to right, up and down and all around, then back again to the test. I do a second one, just in case. I now hold two positive tests, one in each hand. There is no denying the blue stripes, they are there, as plain as day. Boy, this year has taken a turn already and it's only day one! Questions start pouring in all around me, through me, over me. I need to do what I always do when I feel panicked – get outside. I throw on a jumper, a bobble hat, whatever shoes are by the door and grab the dogs' leads. Before I know it I'm pounding the earth. Round and round we go, round the playing field next to our house. I don't feel the cold, or the wet of the grass, I don't hear the kids playing in the playground or the other dog walkers calling their dogs. In fact I don't hear or feel anything. I'm in total shock.

You see, Jim and I had always been careful. For ten years I took the pill. Each and every day until six months ago. I stopped because I'd started to get weird shooting pains running through my legs and they became more frequent. My job involves sitting or standing for hours at a time and when I searched online about leg pains, I didn't like the prognosis.

Thrombosis looked like a possibility for a twenty-six year-old tattoo artist who been on the pill for nearly a decade and I didn't fancy that much. I had done what I do best and looked for an alternative option. Natural Family Planning was it and we embarked on a new adventure of thermometers, spreadsheets and abstaining from sex on 'red days'. It worked! It really was brilliant. I started to understand my body properly for the first time in, well, ever! I started to think, why didn't they teach us this in school? How had I got to twenty six and still not known when I was ovulating? I sure as hell did now! I felt really in control and enjoyed the new knowledge of my body.

Well, we stuck rigidly to no fun on red days, until the 3rd December. This was our ten year anniversary of getting together. We hadn't got married, as we just hadn't got round to it. We'd been far too busy setting up house, our business, travelling and partying to get married. Ten years had flown by in a whirl of ups and downs and all arounds, with us together in the centre. We got drunk and something turned into something-something, you know the way it goes! What's a little carefree loving once in ten years? Well, now here we are, a few weeks later and our world was about to change forever.

I look back on this scene from a further ten years down the line, and I think our Rufus was out there waiting. Waiting for an opportunity, waiting for us to get our act together and open the gate to let him in! The fact we had never chanced it before and on the one time we did, we conceive, is pretty crazy.

I go round the field so many times even the dogs are looking at me like they've had enough. They give me that look like they know what's happening and I should get on with it. But in my mind the questions are piling up. Are we ready? Am I ready? How will our life change? What would this baby do to our relationship? How will we cope at work? What will I do all day? Is this what I want? How? Why? Why not? Funnily, I can visualise in my mind's eye Jim and I with teenagers, but not babies! Is that weird? Maybe that's good. I decide I'm actually going mad and need some food, and then it strikes me: shit! I'm hungover too! Now that opens a mental can of worms. What if I've harmed the baby? Need Google. Time to go in. Jim's still in bed. I make tea. I make toast. I sit for a bit. I breathe. I climb the stairs. It's time.

The next seventy-two hours are a blur. I would love to report that we were really ridiculously happy, but the reality is we were both in shock and we clung together and went round in circles, deliberating over what to do. The reason I am telling everyone this, is precisely the reason I wrote this book, because parenting, from the moment you realise you have a growing foetus inside you, is difficult. It is something that should be thought through and planned for and discussed. Because to parent, is to become a guide. It is to give up on certain journeys and to step up to the plate. It is not something, in my opinion anyway, to enter into without conscious questioning.

So that is what we did. We went back and forth, discussing how we would make it work, and as the reality sunk in, we started to get excited. As time went on, Jim got so excited that he told everyone we knew before we even had a scan! We made a conscious decision together, even though it was after conception. Rufus is definitely supposed to be here. He is one amazing person. I know I am completely biased, but he was a wonderful surprise!

Doesn't life sometimes throw the unexpected at you when you have planned for something else entirely? I wonder how many of you reading this book have experienced something just like that. Such as putting your child into mainstream school, only to find it is not for you. Sheer panic and emotional shock at how your whole life can be turned upside down when your plans do not go quite as expected. Well, I hope this book will give you and your family some relief. Because our life has taken some more unexpected twists and turns, and each time Rufus has been at the centre of it. One thing I know as a parent is that our children are here to guide us, as much as we guide them. I have learnt so, so much from both my children about life and myself and when you realise this and go with it, life has more purpose and it is not such a battle.

So as this book goes on, I ask of you one thing: to read

my words with an open mind. Because if you are to home educate with confidence, an open mind is at the very heart of everything.

It took 3.8 billion years
of triumphant evolution,
remarkable collision,
an unbelievable confluence
made by sheer will and influence
of this infinite universe
and all of the stars
to get you here.

'Miracle', Nikita Gill

Chapter 2
Evolution Takes Place

So the next year was one of expecting, experiencing and falling in love like never before. With each other all over again and with our best collaborative creation yet. Rufus's birth, although fifteen days later than due, was serene. He was born happy, and at nine-and-a-half pounds he was a healthy, bouncy boy. We fell into complete friendship straight away. He was my little mate and I was obsessed from the get-go.

I remember the day it all sunk in. After about four months of being a mum my brain caught up with reality. I was sitting on our bed playing with Ru, and just burst into tears and said, 'I have a son!' Slow on the uptake! But I think motherhood is like this, a constant catching up with what is happening around you; it is so totally absorbing of everything that you are and everything that you feel. Time becomes obsolete for quite a while and your brain just re-programmes and focusses so entirely on your baby, that you forget yourself. Jim and I took to our baby like he had always been with us. We went everywhere together and it was fabulous. Of course I am writing this ten years later, so I am sure my view is a bit rose-tinted! New mums, this is proof that you do indeed forget the sleeplessness and the obliteration of self!

Toddlerhood was the best. We loved watching evolution take place before our eyes, in our own living room! Walking and talking just happened, it felt so natural and we loved it so much that we started talking about having another one. We waited until it felt right and we felt ready, which was another two years down the line, and conceived as easily as we did with Ru. In fact, I knew I was pregnant the very next morning.

Fast forward to November 2011. I had been pregnant for nearly ten months, it felt like forever. I had over-stretched my groin muscles doing too much breaststroke in the pool, and slipping on Rufus's puzzles one morning was not an experience I would wish on my worst enemy. Nothing was starting that labour. I was desperate. I had three unsuccessful sweeps, downed a bottle of castor oil, ate five pineapples in a day, had sex, had curries, had more sex, walked miles, went in the car down a lane with the deepest potholes you have ever seen, holding on for dear life to my bump and the door, still nothing. This pregnancy had been the hardest physical experience of my life. I was done. I was broken. But I was too good-natured to shout and scream. So I waited. I waited too long. I should have shouted and screamed.

On the 29th November our second son Otis was finally born. It was a natural birth, in the birthing pool, but not without complications. He was born a deep blueish purple colour after five minutes of being stuck. We suffered with shoulder dystocia, which is when the shoulders of the baby get stuck in the birth canal, but the head is out. It is not a happy place, for either party. Luckily, I have umbilical cords of steel. This is what kept him alive, that and the fact his head remained under water. There were fifteen people in the room after the alarm had been set off and the silence was only broken by the midwife sobbing on the end of my bed. I had gone into shock and was shaking uncontrollably. The look on my mum's face said what everyone else was thinking: He's dead. Everyone but me. I had been connected to this little thrashing, sensitive soul. I had carried him around for so long, I knew just how darn strong he was. I knew he would be OK. Then we all heard it. It was not a sound I had ever heard before, or again for that matter. You couldn't describe it as a cry; it sounded more like a growl. My little lion, I thought.

I had suffered terribly from stomach muscle separation. Otis had been a big baby. I am not a particularly big person and he weighed in at a whopping ten pounds, fifteen ounces! The midwife on the ward said I might as well have had twins. The surgeon that visited us said it was the worst muscle separation he had ever seen, and I would definitely need surgery. Cheers! Just what I needed to hear at that moment. I very nearly lost my mind that day. That is the closest I have ever come to the edge, the edge of reason, and I very nearly toppled into the abyss of madness. But I clung onto sanity for my boys. That was one of the toughest weeks of my life. But I strapped up my stomach and my non-existent muscles into a bandage corset that the physio gave me, took some deep breaths and made a decision. That I would get on with it. I had to, for my sons. That is what mothers do, we have to after all. I am not a superhero but I am a mum.

This part of my story is important because it is moments like this that make us. It is in the near-loss of our minds and our bodies that we understand why we are here. The traumatic experience on that day has helped me find strength in myself again and again, because if I could get up and get on after that birth, then I can pretty much do anything! I have found learning in the pain and the trauma of that day and it has actually stood me in good stead for things to come. I have unravelled the experience and consciously tuned it to 'I can handle this' which is a good mantra for any parent to have! Finding the raw, deep part of me that day that very nearly lost it, actually enabled growth, and a strength I did not know was possible. Pain and trauma can be seen as the worst things ever, but they can also be the beginnings of a different entity of self. One who can stand tall and know for sure that she achieved the unthinkable, got through the experience and is still very much alive and tuned into life because of it. All mothers, no matter the birth experience, should honour themselves in this conscious awareness for it sets us up for greatness and the belief that, 'we got this!'

I loved having a baby again. Otis was so much fun – another happy smiler who loved his food and fresh-air walks in the sling. In fact, he pretty much lived on my back for the first two years. Whether I was hoovering, cooking, painting or reading Rufus bedtime stories, Otis was there with me, literally strapped to me.

After about a year, I found the name for the type of

parents we were. A book about 'Attachment Parenting' pretty much described how we went about our days and our nights. I had already learnt about the importance of attachment while reading about developmental psychology. Attachment is key to providing a safe space to grow and develop, without being in a constant state of insecurity or fear. It teaches a child how to love and be loved, which is extremely important for the rest of their lives.

I remember as a child in the 1980s, watching the horrific images on the evening news of Romanian orphanages. Under the dictator Ceauşescu, Romanian children were subjected to mass incarceration, in state institutions where they were emotionally and physically abused. Small children were left in cots with no touch or kindness from their so-called caregivers, and on the television footage, you could see they had something missing (studies on these children – now adults – have shown the long-term effect on their mental health). This is an extreme and harrowing example, but it provides food for thought.

Attachment has a major influence on effective regulation of feelings as an adult, so if a child is abused or neglected by their primary caregiver, they may develop a lifelong problem with forming attachments of any kind. In my confidence coaching work, I see these detrimental impacts on a person's life, all the way into their thirties and forties.

Most home educators I have met fit this sort of parenting – conscious and affectionate with their kids. I think this is why they are more likely to have issues with the very early start that the UK government suggests that children have at school. At age four or five a child is at an important age for attachment, and being torn away from each other causes much insecurity for parents and children.

As Rufus turned three, the reality of school started to turn up on our radar. He had been attending preschool one day a week from the age of one. After a while, he went in OK. He seemed to have fun and was smiley when we picked him up. I went back to work once a week and this gave me opportunities to not only make some money, but to be creative and talk to adults! I enjoyed my day at work, but I loved picking up Ru more. He completed me.

After Otis was born we started to look into schools more seriously, and began thinking about moving closer to where I had grown up, as the village schools were smaller than those in the larger suburb where we lived. As I look back now, this was my attempt at trying to control the situation, a situation I knew very little about, apart from my own experiences. They were not particularly great; I remembered some good times at school, but I had strong memories of being bullied and feeling very alone. I was attempting to find a quaint school from the movies, somewhere my Rufus would be safe, and in my mind this was a country school, with a village backdrop!

We set a plan in motion. The house got white-washed, the 'for sale' sign went up, and we moved into my mum's house. I could not deal with trying to keep the house spotless for potential buyers, with two little boys and two dogs in it. That way we could enrol Ru at a local school while we looked for a suitable house nearby. Again, life twisted on us and things did not go exactly as I envisioned. We did find a house, but it needed a lot of renovation, plus it took a long time to complete the paper work. All in all, it took us two years to get the place liveable. But that is life.

I believe this house was waiting for us, and we had to earn it. We are grateful every day that we wake up here, and love every day we spend here. It has taken blood, sweat and a whole lot of tears to make it home, but it is ours. But much has changed since we moved in five years ago.

We never considered not sending our boys to school. We did not know that we had a choice. Our knowledge about home educating was very limited; I thought it was for really religious people or families living in the Australian outback. I remember watching an episode of the TV programme *Wife Swap* which featured a couple living in a converted bus with their two children who were unschooled, and the programme made it seem that they were quite ignorant. The new 'swapped' wife got the kids reading and writing and was made out to be an evangelical teacher. The kids enjoyed her lessons and it made the 'hippy' parents seem silly. I remember thinking how I would definitively want my kids to be able to read and write but sadly I did not think on it long enough.

What I know now is that home educating is a subtle art; it cannot be properly conveyed on an edited TV programme, because so much happens at once, and yet it can appear as though nothing is happening because it does not look like our conditioned perception of learning (as school does). But when we think about how home-educating unschoolers live, they are learning through experience all the time. They are enabled through curiosity rather than being taught, so the learning is so much deeper and more real. The children are choosing what to learn and not being forced to sit and take part, when their brain can quite easily switch off and be numb to the experience, though they are still seemingly partaking of the lesson.

I look back at these preschool years now and realise how ignorant and conditioned Jim and I were and I feel silly for not having the forethought to see what's what. Sometimes we have to learn the hard way in life and that is what happened.

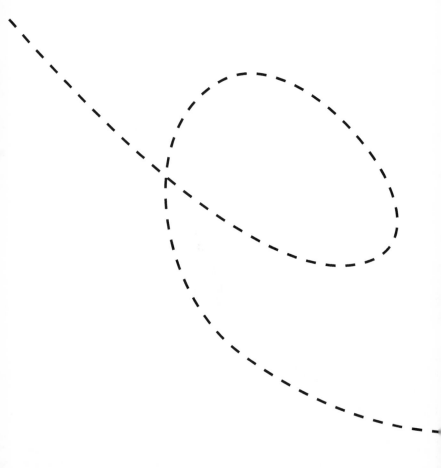

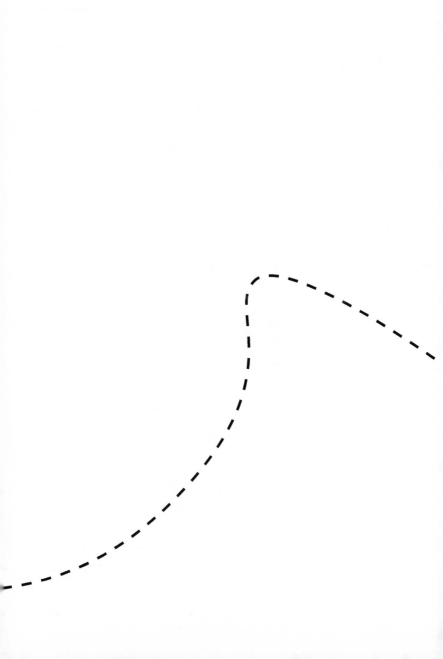

Children are not only extremely good at learning; they are much better at it than we are.

John Holt

Chapter 3
At the School Gates

Rufus's first day at school came round. He had a place in a village school, which had one class per year. It looked great; new buildings, a big field and seemingly lots of good facilities – gym equipment and the like. I did not really know what to look for in a school, so I treated it much the same as looking for a house. I went on gut feelings and it felt good! We met the teacher and she seemed like a rational human being, albeit young and rather inexperienced. Rufus's class was to be her first. But, we thought, everyone starts somewhere and maybe as she was a child not that long ago, she would have insight into the children's needs. Perhaps she had boundless energy and would be fun.

On that first day, Rufus was shy, so shy and clinging onto me. I went in with him and the grip got tighter. It felt wrong and yet I pushed him away. I can see his little face now, pleading 'Don't leave me' but saying it just with his eyes. Then came an ambiguous look of distrust as I backed away and said, 'It's only until lunchtime!' In the back of my mind, just out of my conscious awareness, was a belief that school was for the best for the family and this had to happen. I believed that it was supposed to be hard, to feel wrong, but you did it anyway! Rather than confront this belief I submitted to it, and went through the motions in a trance, to avoid the pain of letting go of my child far too early.

Rufus made new friends and we all settled into the new routine, sort of. I say sort of, because Jim and I experienced the weird feeling of not actually being in control of when we left our house in the morning, when we ate or when we slept, because of this new obligation. We started our own business when we were in our early twenties and have called the shots in our life ever since, so for us this imposed structure was uncomfortable. We assumed this feeling would dissipate.

Rufus carried on. Some days he would moan a bit and I would hustle him in the morning, but on the whole the Reception year went OK. Our first parents' evening was good. Sitting at the tiny tables, surrounded by colourful pictures and baskets of cool-looking things made me feel better. It is strange how parents are not often welcomed into schools; it is such a huge contrast from preschool, where generally you are made to feel a part of it, through the ritual of drop-offs and pick-ups, and there is an ongoing conversation.

But schools have gates and fences to keep the parents out. We all assume it is to keep the children in, but I think it is for the first reason. Pick-ups and drop-offs were interesting times. At first, everyone was friendly and there was a feeling of camaraderie for a few weeks, but then the cliques began to form. I watched on with interest; it was like a social study, as some circles of parents turned their backs to others. The schoolyard really was a backdrop for social conflicts, eye-rolling and disingenuous gossip. Being a bit quirky-looking anyway, and not bothered about fitting in, I did not participate in any clique and was very happy to remain on the fringes of schoolyard society, where I probably belong. I am too far along my path to be interested in anything other than authenticity.

School holidays came round and we loved it. We were all together again and the feeling of completeness came back. We could spend time as we wanted, even if that was jumping in puddles in onesies and eating cake on the trampoline. A dark shadow crept over the last day, and as we arranged the packed lunch and uniform we all knew what was coming to us once again. I have a saying now, that you can tell if you are a home educator by the way you feel when term time resumes. If you feel relief that finally the kids are back to school, then perhaps it is not for you! I felt darkness in my soul. I felt resolute that it had to happen though, so I could get back to work. I was kidding myself and once again living unconsciously through conditioning. Ru went back quietly, as he always did, before he knew there was a choice. I tried my best to hype up all the positives, as I did, before I knew there was a choice. And we somehow carried on.

It really started to get hard after the spring half term. Rufus would start every day distressed, worrying over his socks or scratchy trousers, and he became a master in avoiding getting his uniform on. I would be stressing out, as one eye on the clock told me the minutes were ticking by, and I felt all the pressure of time upon us. I would get shouty and chaotic, running around like a blue-arsed fly. Rufus would be argumentative, hyper and eventually sad. This new pattern began out of nowhere and became our go-to behaviour each morning. I tried pre-empting it, and do things differently, but to no avail. Once we had got Rufus in the car, on the way to school there would always be tears. I saw him change as a person. I would drop him off and I could see him breaking. The look of disdain on his face as he accepted his fate. He would slowly walk in and give fake smiles. He was learning to wear a mask; he was pretending to be OK, when really he was far from it.

After school, we would see the angst. The anger would fire up out of him, as if it had been repressed all day. He had been so good and so quiet all day, and the rage had to come out. He would rage at his little brother, he would kick the doors, he would shout at me until the exhaustion got the best of him and finally he would give in and be Rufus again, until the next morning. This battle, this cycle carried on. I went into the school a few times, to check that he was OK in class time, and this concern was met with vague looks of misunderstanding and assurances that Rufus was a quiet boy, but well behaved. Followed by remarks about how he really should try to put his hand up more in class. I sat back and observed. On Friday evenings there was relief and on Monday mornings a tantrum. Rages throughout the week on school nights, but nothing on weekends. We were rolling along towards summer and the new term brought another parents' evening our way.

I waited in the hallway, looking around at all the painted

self-portraits. I smiled to myself as I imagined being a kid again and seeing the world through their eyes. I noticed how all the portraits were really smiling and also how they were all dressed in school colours. I wondered what the brief might have been. 'Alright children, we want a happy self-portrait and make sure you're dressed in your lovely school uniforms!' I imagined the teacher checking over their shoulders and getting them to make the smiles bigger. Was the colourful cheerfulness all a façade?

I heard my name. My turn. Into the classroom I went. The Year One room certainly had fewer cool things in baskets, but there was an underwater corner and a sink evidently used for paints, so that made me feel better. I sat down opposite Rufus's teacher. It was the same teacher from Registration year; she had gained some experience and had followed the class up through the school. I thought this would be a good thing as she should really know my boy, after having spent so long in his company.

I was met with an academic low-down and shown a visual of an 'average line', which she remarked Rufus was quite below. I still do not know what average they were using. Were they equating the children's academic prowess at five or six against a world average? A local average? I'm guessing it was a national average, but come on, they are six years old! How can that be a rational way to judge anything?

She started to talk about dyslexia and mentioned possible testing. She lost me at that point. I remember interrupting her – 'How is he getting on in the class? Does he seem happy? Does he have a set group he hangs out with? What's he like in P.E.?' She looked at me with the same vague misunderstanding from before. I clarified, 'To be honest, I don't really care where he's at academically, he's six!' I think I lost her at that point. We were two women, sitting across a small table in a classroom, but we might as well have been on different continents, speaking different languages.

I tried to bring it back on track by asking to see some artwork. After all, we are artists, and I wanted to see some evidence of creativity happening. This was something that had obviously not been prepped but she went off into a cupboard to find something to show the crazy arty mother! I sat there wondering what the point of it all was. Why did parents come to parents' evening at primary school? It cannot be to find out where their sons or daughters are plotted on the average line, surely? Was it? I had the strong feeling that I had got the wrong end of the stick, and perhaps there should be a manual for this kind of teacher-parent etiquette. Then she flopped back into her chair and dropped some pages of beautiful drawings onto the desk in front of me. She remarked how Rufus was quite an artist and his drawings had been chosen to represent his class, alongside another pupil's, in the hallway. Wow! I thought, and you weren't even going to mention that were you?

I left the parents' evening in a confused state, none the wiser about the goings on behind the school gates. The average line, that red line on the page, haunted me. I thought, I don't want my kid to be plotted on an average line. I want to pull that line off that page and wave it around my head and throw it into the sky. Fuck average, I thought in my rebellious, arty mind. I thought about all the plans and dreams we had set out for our children, and they certainly never involved an average line.

I drove home through the lanes thinking about the things Jim and I had discussed in those hazy days of early pregnancy. We had gone over everything, including school, and we had been resolute back then that school would not be enough, that we would top up their knowledge with real-world learning and experiences. This sparked something inside me. A seed of a thought was sown on that drive home that would soon begin to grow, quickly develop and bloom into a plan. But not yet.

As the summer term began, Rufus became more restless each day. We had the same stressful mornings, him begging and avoiding and using itchy trousers as an excuse not to get dressed. There were headaches, stomach aches, sore throats, pretending to be sick and other imaginative but obvious techniques at bunking off school. By this point, Jim refused to take Ru to school. He found it too distressing and went to work depressed and saddened by his boy's unhappiness.

I had begun to research some alternatives. Starting with other schools, different types of school, home education. I initially looked up the law, as I had literally no clue what it was. Considering that you can get fined for taking your kid on holiday during term time, I assumed it would involve jumping through lots of legal hoops. I was pleasantly surprised when I looked up my local government's webpage and read the actual law:

> The parent of every child of compulsory school age shall cause him to receive efficient full-time education suitable –

(a) to his age, ability and aptitude, and
(b) to any special educational needs he may have, either by regular attendance at school or otherwise. (Education Act, 1996)

Oh, I thought. This is interesting. I was actually proud of the freedom that this seemed to point to. Was our state actually this lenient? Perhaps we are not in an Orwellian surveillance society after all! This revelation gave nutrients to the seed and things really started to line up. Jim and I began discussing home education. I really needed him on board if this was going to work. I need not have worried – he had been convinced back in the spring with the tadpoles fiasco.

For show-and-tell one Friday, Rufus, with Jim by his side, had proudly taken in a big jar of tadpoles. Every year of the boys' lives we have had tadpoles, carefully brought inside to a fish tank, and we have marvelled at nature's creative design. Rufus knew about tadpoles. The whole class had been so excited by this show-and-tell that Jim suggested to the teachers that he could set up a tank for the classroom. They were not over the moon with the idea, but when he said he would clean it, and take the creatures away as they turned into frogs, they agreed. After a week or so he went in to check on the tadpoles, and there above the tank was a big poster, handdrawn by the teachers. To Jim's horror, the cycle of the tadpole to frog was wrong. They had drawn tadpoles with front legs before they developed back legs. This was monumental for Jim, who likes things black and white, right or wrong. He concluded that school was not always right. The fact that Rufus knew the tadpole cycle but had to learn it incorrectly, was the last straw.

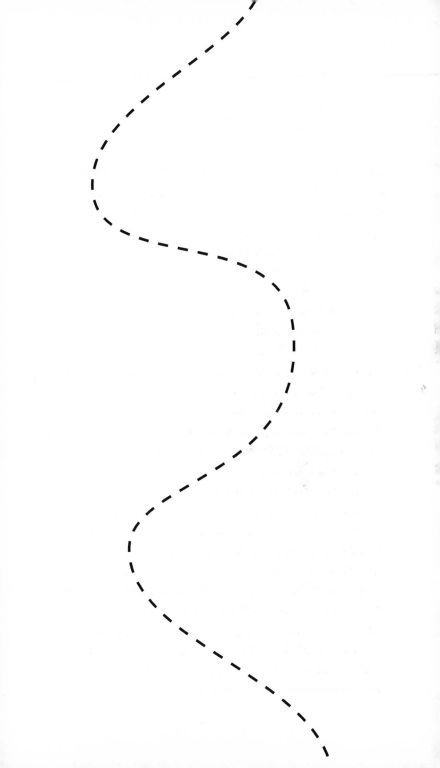

Children are not things to be moulded, but people to be unfolded

Jess Lair

Chapter 4
The Day We Left the System

We were having a usual school day morning. Rufus was playing up and I was running around in a stressed, near-exhausted whirlwind of huffs and puffs. I passed his bedroom in a flurry of over-hyped energy as I attempted to inject some of it into every part of the house, trying to get the boys out of the door and into the car. I stopped dead. The scene that lay before me was my six-year-old, standing at his desk with a pair of big kitchen scissors, cutting up his school jumper, saying under his breath, 'I'm not going, I fucking hate school!' He was taking big chunks out of his uniform as he said it again and again.

My mind took a second to process what I was seeing and my mouth spoke too soon – or rather, shouted. 'RUFUS!' He looked up in panic, dropped the tatters of his school clothes and ran past me into the bathroom and locked the door, shouting 'I'm not going!' through the door once more. At last my brain worked out it was probably best not to shout and I tried to calmly say through the door things like 'Come on Ru', and 'Let's talk about this'. Still nothing. I could hear sobs. My heart was breaking. Jim was there with me and as we tried to prise Ru out, my mind was playing the game of 'think the worst'. I could not see the scissors anywhere, so I started to think he might have them in the loo with him.

Jim and I had planned to talk about home education with Rufus soon. We were going to sit down and explain everything and put in place how it might work etc. But that day, life was proving once again that it was not going to stick to our schedule.

Finally we heard the bathroom lock click. I turned the handle and saw my little boy, red faced and big eyed. I stretched out my arms: 'Come here'. He fell into them, 'Sorry Mum'. No, I thought, I'm sorry! But I said, 'It's OK, but I think we need to sit down and talk about this. You don't have to go to school today, but we need to have an important chat'.

At first, he thought he was in trouble, but I just wanted to calm him down. I did not want him to think that he got his way because he cut up his uniform – I needed to reframe the whole thing and look at the bigger picture. Now I can see the funny side. I mean, how punk rock is my kid?

Jim, Ru and I sat at the kitchen table and our son waited for a lecture. We just came out with it. 'We've been looking at alternatives to going to school Ru, and we've found out about something called home education, where you can do all your learning with us at home'. His little eyes brightened. 'You will still need to do school work, but in a different way. We need to look into it some more, but if you want to try, then we're happy to give it a go'. Rufus was smiling, and it was not his fake smile, it was the real Rufus one. 'Yes please!'

What happened next, no-one could have predicted. Ru wanted to get books out and begin! He wrote his name on the front of some exercise books I had bought when I had been out shopping, just in case. He then wrote subject names on the front. He was so focussed and busy with it all. 'How do you spell science Mum?'

The energy that kid had that morning was infectious. I set about looking up de-registration; I had seen a template letter online and wanted to copy it out. I joined some Facebook groups that were run by local home-edders. They were all private groups, so I had to wait to be accepted before I could look at the info.

On day two I went into the school. I met the Headmaster and explained what we wanted to do. He was not surprised and even seemed quite supportive. He had heard how we had brought in tadpoles and had also joined the crowd which gathered to watch Rufus and Jim's papier-mâché and Mentos volcano erupt in the playground during one show-and-tell. He had seen evidence that we were into this parenting lark and were up to the challenge. I gave him the letter, he wished us luck and said he would contact the local authority ... and that was it. As I closed the tall metal gate for the last time I felt emotional. I looked back once more and then strode to my car. I could have skipped but I thought they might be watching!

That first week went by so fast. In fact the whole month did! Looking back from where we are now and what we know now, it seems like a different life. We were so naive and new. We were raw from the traumas of those school-day mornings and sad experiences. Our family needed to reboot and repair, but we wanted to throw all our energy into this new chapter and try and focus on how we were going to educate our child, rather than take our time.

This is one of the things you learn as you go on. As a home educator, time is on your side, but you do not comprehend this at first. Some of us are conditioned to believe that a day starts at a certain time, that there are optimum hours for brain function or concentration, or even just routines that need respect. This usually creates some learning experiences for new home educators – believe me, we went through a lot of learning, and I do not mean the kids!

When you look more seriously and closely at home educating, there are so many paths to consider and many options. You come across ideas about curriculums, different theorists and approaches, and entirely new words – like 'Unschoolers' for example. I didn't find this word for a while though.

In the meantime, through all of this, Otis was going to preschool. It was a wonderful, open plan, play outside whatever the weather kind of place. He went for three sessions each week and loved it. I had joined the committee and got involved, even painting some murals on the walls of the 'seaside room'. The manager Jo had the idea to fill an indoor room with sand to make a beach. I mean, what's not to like about that?

So in the beginning, we set about doing school from home, as many folks do. We had a routine: when Otis went to preschool we sat down and started some maths workbooks, or attempted a science experiment from a guide or YouTube tutorial. We read school-like books and practiced writing. At first it was cool. After all, we were not having the tantrums or stress like a couple of months before. All that was so fresh in our minds, and this seemed so much better.

Jim and I were planning to get married that June, so there were lots of things to think about and organise. Rufus came with us to meetings with the lovely Humanist Celebrant who was to perform the marriage – and who turned out to be a big fan of home education. This is learning, I thought. And it started to sink in that every experience in life is. The wedding was fantastic, a great day in our back garden with lots of friends and family. Our sons sat with us under the magnolia tree and acted as ring bearers. I noticed how much more chilled Rufus was. His shoulders had dropped and that gorgeous smile made a lot of appearances. We were able to tell a lot of people about our new education choice and their responses were interesting. It was also the summer holidays by then and it did not feel like we should be at school anyway, so we set about enjoying summer in the knowledge that when September came around we would be free.

New friends

When the new term arrived, Rufus and I started going to some home education groups. And on the days he was at home, Otis joined us. Rufus was quite shy and still took a while to warm up. Oti on the other hand was straight in there, which seemed to help Ru follow in after. This sparked something in three-year-old Otis. A lot of his buddies had left preschool to go up to Registration year, he was coming out with us half the week and knew Rufus was at home, and he said he wanted to try home school too! It made sense really to have both at home, so I told the preschool and out he came.

Meeting other home educators is the best. You go in to meet-ups feeling a bit unsure, not knowing what to expect, and are usually met by a gaggle of confident kids who say hello and make eye contact, even with adults! The mums seem to be less uptight than school mums, and put much less emphasis on what they look like too. Conversations tend to be about education, kids, crafts, and the new things they are trying.

I felt such a relief when we attended that first group. I met my good friend Vicky for the first time that day. Her son William had come out of school almost to the day that Rufus had, and we got on straight away. She was in the same boat and we were not sinking! It was great to hear all of her thoughts and ideas. We went over our reasons and experiences, telling each other how we had had enough with the system that was school. We were perhaps idealistic but only through necessity.

I also met a woman called Jane who had two sons. When I asked when they had started home schooling, she said, 'We always have!' 'So your boys have never been to school?' 'No!' Wow, here was a woman I needed to get to know, how inspiring. 'Do your boys read?' I asked somewhat naively, but actually wanting to know if they did. She told me how her son Tom had taught himself to read and was now a complete bookworm. I smiled. I felt at home in this crowd. The children were freer, the parents were more relaxed and no one shouted at their kids the whole time we were there. It felt like a veil had been lifted and I was at last seeing another side, a parallel world that

I was not previously aware of.

I had ordered a lot of different books on education, learning theories and different teaching methods and was ferociously reading everything I could. A few years before, I had studied psychology at Adult Education, and had learnt about developmental psychology and how we learn and retain information, but this was ramping it up to a new level. I was reading about how kids were OK without the prescribed ways of learning in orthodox education, and it made me feel like we could break out of the box, and carry on as we did before school got in the way.

It made sense that my kids did not fit into the system. When I looked at our lifestyle and what my kids had been born into and brought up with until school age, I felt a bit silly for even thinking that they would fit! Jim and I are freethinkers, we are artist business-owners who have challenged the typical lifestyle, we have travelled quite extensively and we question authority and everything around us. We do not accept knowledge until we have thought it over and we certainly do not always do as we are told! We are a couple who stand up for our own beliefs and like to debate the whys and wheres of history and politics. We draw, paint, and make stuff. Our house is full of curios and random objects and we love being outside. I started to think that I was mad to even try to put a child of ours into mainstream school. The more I considered it, the more home education seemed like the path for us, forever!

Learning all the time
Through this research, I was not becoming an expert in teaching, but I was fast becoming an expert on my own

opinion of teaching! How you teach or impart knowledge to a child is so specific to how that individual uses their own senses, and therefore teaching is easier when you know the child and you control the environment they learn in.

At school there are so many children, so many variables. At home, it is home. It is an amazing, stable base to begin learning from. After all, your children have learnt from this base since they were born! To think that we only begin to learn properly once we are taken out of our home environment and put into a schoolroom is crazy. In fact, I now believe that, in some individuals, that move can completely incapacitate learning. It can create so much anxiety and heightened stimulation that it hinders the learning process.

When the mind goes into that 'fight or flight' mode, scared and adrenalized, we are not in the best position to take in information, or think about anything other than simply surviving. Our brain waves become incoherent and we cannot retain focus or memorise information. Our body undergoes stress and our digestion is affected. If our emotional response is denied for a long time, it will develop into physical symptoms of dis-ease. This might be skin irritations, allergies, ulcers, migraines or anything from an endless list of symptoms.

I am not just school-bashing. In certain families school is a blessing. Its routines provide some families with stability, a hot meal and other children and adults as role models and a source of support and help. Schools try and succeed in helping many families.

Teachers are not the enemy either. All the teachers I

have met outside of their day jobs are articulate and full of energy to make a difference. I think they are the people who are the most let down by the current system, as they cannot teach the way they wish to. I know one wonderful woman, a primary school teacher, who pours so much of herself into her career, but is met with misunderstanding, jealousy, or red tape and bureaucracy at every turn. She wishes she could be free to do her best job for the kids she adores and wants the best for. In the existing state school system, each step is painstakingly evaluated and reconsidered and argued, and changes take too long. Meanwhile, years are going by and our children are being let down.

The way I see it, schools begin a process of conditioning, making our kids believe that to succeed, or experience success, they have to prove their worth over and over again. They are constantly tested, examined, checked and graded. In some schools they are 'streamed', divided and ranked. And this all takes place within a hierarchical environment (like our wider society) which puts kids at the bottom. Opinions or ideas that do not align with the majority vote are not praised, they are oppressed and forgotten, or even disciplined out. All this dramatically reduces the children's self-worth.

I know this sounds like quite a harsh viewpoint, but I am not alone in this opinion. Books by John Holt and John Taylor Gatto (the Two Johns, as I like to call them) have helped me understand what schooling is, and how it is not enough. Holt and Gatto were both revered educators who came to the conclusion that mass schooling is not the way forward any more. They both appeal to the radical side of me and my non-conformist ideals.

John Holt was an early advocate of unschooling who coined the phrase 'learning all the time'. This was also the name of his 1989 book, about how children learn, how they explore the world around them and how they create their own knowledge from connections, questions and experiences. Significantly, it was written in the 1980s before the spread of the internet in every household. Holt emphasises how a child's learning merely needs facilitating, rather than directing. I like this theory.

John Taylor Gatto is a man I fell in love with on YouTube. He is a great hulk of a man, with a broad and deep voice. Everything he says is insightful. Jim and I sat and watched an epic five-hour filmed interview with him over two evenings and felt totally enlightened and validated by the end of it. The documentary is called *The Ultimate History Lesson: A Weekend with John Taylor Gatto* (directed by Richard Andrew Grove, 2012), and I highly recommend you watch it if you are interested in the history of education, home education or unschooling, and want to know why and how we are all conditioned.

Gatto was a school teacher for nearly thirty years, in both state and private schools, who saw his students as individuals. He won numerous awards for his teaching in New York City, and then famously resigned from his post by printing the resignation letter in the Wall Street Journal, stating that his role as a teacher was hurting children. Gatto believed that, if enabled and facilitated as an individual, everyone can find their passion in life and become fulfilled, without a school system in place. He was an educational activist, and urged parents to take control of their children's learning rather than leave it up to the state.

In the film, Gatto explains the politically-motivated processes used in public schools across the globe. It helped me unravel the background to mass schooling, and theorise more clearly why unschooling and 'open-source' learning is the better choice.

His main arguments are as follows: Mainstream schooling lacks any personal input or choice about what you are learning. Public schooling suppresses individual curiosity and self-mastery. Public schooling teaches through memorisation, which leads to confusion. (A quick side-note: Because he was American, Gatto refers to 'public schooling' while in Britain we call it 'state schooling'.)

Gatto believed that education is a function, not a profession. Rather than a job which starts and stops when the bell rings, it is something that everyone does all of the time, and everything is educational. Public schooling makes children emotionally dependent on approval from authority. It teaches a kind of self-confidence called 'provisional self-esteem', which requires constant confirmation from experts or authority. In schools, constant surveillance is normalised, which sets children up for life in a society where surveillance of our information, data, and person is widespread.

This is all a real eye-opener. In fact, all of John Taylor Gatto's books and interviews are incredibly inspirational and inform all sorts of debate and re-thinking. John T. G. passed away the year I wrote this book, 2018. He was a marvel and I wholly recommend all his work.

Learn something because you need it, or because you love it.

Charles Aldrich

Chapter 5
Unschooling

The day I found unschooling was a breakthrough moment in my development as a mum, as a woman, as a human! I was reading Sandra Dodd's *Book of Unschooling* and a light bulb, or actually more like a floodlight, went on in my mind. This was it! Oh, how it made sense. It was so obvious and yet my conditioning and others' beliefs had hidden it from me. Unschooling was the most natural way to learn. It is not easy to pinpoint exactly what unschooling is, but I like Sandra's definition, that 'from the point of view of the parent, it is creating and maintaining an environment in which natural learning flourishes'.

Within the unschooling community, there are a number of different factions or variants, with Radical Unschoolers as the most committed to the approach. This means no formal learning of any kind. So no workbooks, no curated lessons, just open-ended, child-led curiosity, and whole-life learning. The word 'radical' includes the meanings progressive and thorough, and this is how I see it, as a committed lifestyle. This makes it quite different from the way most people live in contemporary society.

In *Unschooling Rules*, Clark Aldrich remarks that, 'diverse exposure is part of a rich life'. He means that, in an unschooling lifestyle, a child is immersed in a rich learning environment. Out in the world, instead of stuck in a classroom, learning takes place because it is impossible for it not to. When encouraged and guided by the adults in their lives, unschoolers cannot help but become 'curiouser and curiouser!' And just as Alice did in Wonderland, they will open their minds and their hearts to a lifelong journey of self-discovery and a love of learning.

Unschooling is radically different from what we conventionally believe learning is, once we reach school age. But as babies it is what we do: we learn and take in information from our environment. As unschoolers, we hold on to that infant's desire to explore. We find things that particularly interest us, and spend time practicing and almost obsessing over them until we are done and move onto something new. We are open to everything around us. We are naturally curious and so we want to learn, experience and develop. Time is just a concept, and we follow much more natural rhythms. Unschooling follows a child's unique pace rather than a set of enforced beliefs about what they should be doing at a certain point in their development.

However, unschooling is not for the faint of heart. It is not something to simply have a go at. It is a big commitment to a whole lifestyle, and is impossible to do half-heartedly. Starting unschooling has got to be a conscious decision and everyone needs to be on board and understanding of the goal. Focussing on how to do this as a family is a priority, and a good length of time needs to be spent 'deschooling' first.

Now, when you read this as a new home educator just out of the school system, or as somebody considering this path, you will feel one of two things: scared, or excited. Or perhaps a mixture of the two! If you are excited - brilliant, you should be, because you are about to embark on a journey of self-discovery and start a whole new life away from the 'normal'. You are about to emerge from The Box! This can feel scary at first because you are taking a leap of faith. You feel responsible for your children and this decision affects you all. But so does school! And for whatever reason, school is not working so you are being conscious, responsible and courageous. Rather than allowing your life to roll along in negative submission you are taking control. It may feel overwhelming as you make the decision, but once it is done you can get on with your life and explore what it can become.

The gift of time and freedom

I was reading about how we might live like this as children, teens and adults, and it seemed perfect to me. I was excited by the fact that unschooling meant no timeframe, or to flip that around, all-the-time frame! I began to really absorb the concept that everything is learning and it is impossible not to learn. My mind opened to this readily, and I saw that it was actually another level of freedom. I have always been about feeling liberated and this opened all the doors. I was so excited by the possibilities of unschooling, that I could not wait to wake up the next day and start.

The next few months went by and we felt great. We made more home-ed friends and had lots of fun. We visited museums, parks, woods, beaches, London and Scotland. We did all the mundane everyday life stuff together, like going to the bank, post office, library, supermarket etc. We planted our garden, walked our dogs, visited friends and family, cleaned our house and messed it up again with science experiments, painting and crafts, and various imaginary games.

We lived a life predominantly without time restrictions or rules other than our own moral standards, and we learnt constantly. Once you stop labelling learning and you start living by the unschooling method, you soon realise it is far too time consuming, and rather impossible, to log or keep tabs on when/what you are learning. Far too much happens. There is so much conversation about everything! 'Where do baked beans come from? What's the tin made of? Why are they orange? How many go into a can? Are they good for you? What's digestion?' etc etc etc. The minds of children – and also adults – are so curious and full of questions that it is impossible not to learn.

Now, the argument against this sort of learning is that all this is not necessarily important information. My counter argument is to question, 'Who gets to decide that?' Is it the child who wants to know more about the world they live in, or a bureaucrat somewhere in government that gets to set the standard knowledge for us all? A child may want lots of information on baked beans one day as he or she is testing and developing knowledge of their environment. The next day this could be, 'Why do we have cables going into our house?' or 'How does the petrol in the car make it go?'

The biggest advantage of this style of learning is that it is relevant, real and current. Because it is always happening, it creates a momentum of mind. By this, I mean that the child is creating a way of thinking that is progressive and always growing. Traditional methods such as rote learning, like learning spellings and times-tables by heart, or being tested on certain facts, teach children to memorise and regurgitate information, not create it or question it.

In today's world, the population is at an all-time high, the percentage of university graduates is the highest in history, and robotics and artificial intelligence are soon to become normality. We do not need a society full of people able to memorise. What we need is a generation of free-thinking, creative, self-managing, multi-tasking minds able to deal with an ever-changing technological future. Anyway, some facts come and go. So many things that were taught as fact twenty years ago are now proved wrong, as we make new discoveries about atoms, epigenetics, quantum physics, the universe, and everything!

The internet has changed our world so dramatically in such a short space of time that what is taught in schools today is obsolete already for tomorrow's marketplace. The world is increasingly entrepreneurial and the way to make money and create a life in the future will not rely on one's ability to pass exams. There may no longer be a nine-to-five day, or a career that will span a lifetime.

In fact, people from the millennial generation are swapping their roles in the workplace as often as every two years already. Loyalty to corporations is over. The era of the freelancer and entrepreneurial creative is upon us. Multiple careers with multiple income streams is ever more possible. I know many people who earn their living from their passion – hobbies that turned into careers through a good use of social media, technology and time management.

To have the time and freedom as a child to find out what you are interested in and passionate about is a gift. I believe this is the premise and purpose of unschooling. Children who are able to try things and decide what they love to do, without the limits of timetables or routines, will find their passion in life. They will be able to focus and obsess about things that interest them, and that is precisely how you practice and become able and competent. Following their passions also boosts their self-confidence, awareness and a sense of responsibility. This is what I want for my kids. This is want I want for myself. This is, in fact, what I want for our world.

So, we are unschoolers. We do not have a set routine. But we do not live a completely unruly life. Well, some people might think we do if they dropped into our house at any given moment, but if they stay for a while they will be able to see the method in the apparent madness. When people who do not home educate ask me what my week is like, I cannot answer, because in all honesty every week in our life is different.

Some things happen every week, and so the other goings-on are structured around those. For example I go into the tattoo studio twice a week, so Jim is with the boys on those days. On Sunday and Monday we are all together. The boys go to certain clubs that run at a set time each week. At the moment they love going to the Mixed Martial Arts gym and doing jujitsu, they also swim, visit skate parks, and Rufus and Jim mountain bike together. But I am very open that this could all change at any time.

There have been lots of things that we have tried for a few months then decided to drop and I am fine with that, because my whole outlook values experiences. This causes some debate with parents, and with people in general for that matter. Within the school system, the thought is that you have paid for a term's worth of clubs, so those kids are going. Or you have enrolled in Scouts or Cubs and there is an unwritten expectation of loyalty. My Rufus never got this! He has tried many things and some have stuck and he loves them to this day, and others have fallen by the wayside.

Kids should not have to commit, in my opinion. I know this is controversial, but it is our conditioning that tells us they should! I remember one opinion that stuck with me when I said that we were going to take Ru out of school. When asked why, I said, 'because it's not working for him, he's sad and isn't happy in school', and she said, 'but if you take him out, how will he learn that life is full of stuff we don't want to do, but have to?' I thought, wow! He is a little kid! He has a right to his happiness, a right to find himself, and a right to try things and decide if he likes them or not.

But the more I thought about this reaction I thought how poignant it was. If you believe that life is full of stuff we do not want to do, but have to do anyway, then what is the point? To me, the point is the good stuff, the stuff that we jump out of bed each morning to do, the stuff that gets our heart racing, our mind whirling, our emotions fired up, that creates an insatiable hunger for more. Then we get on with the other stuff, like going to the bank, doing the food shopping and cleaning the house because that is a choice too.

Forcing a child to commit to things they do not enjoy does not make them responsible or committed, it makes them depressed. Perhaps that is what is wrong with a lot of people though; perhaps they did not have the opportunity to find their passion in life or they believed they had to slog too hard to make it. That is another conditioned belief and one that gets built by a system that is not geared up for individual empowerment.

Habits and routines

As a remedial hypnotist, I see people struggling with depression and anxiety all the time. In nearly all cases, they are stuck in a cycle of thinking that confirms their belief that they are not good enough. We are told as children, or we assume as children, that we are not good enough because we are tested and we fail. We are made examples of, and we are embarrassed. We are pitted against each other, and we become competitors, so once again, we sometimes fail. Rather than finding what makes us feel good and confident in our abilities or our interests, we carry on day after day, slogging on for years. At the end, we come out with some test results and a broken will.

This sounds really negative, and I know some people relish the academic system and find their passion in mathematics, science or literature and for them I am truly happy, but there are many others who do not. These are the people who see me later in life, after years of battling with low self-esteem and the belief that they are not worth it. It is not their fault, and I help them find something to do that interests them, because it is when we discover something that we are passionate about that we want to put in the practice and the hard work, because we feel alive and excited.

Fulfilment comes from having something in your life that you feel is important and worth doing. Empowerment comes from knowing your own worth and feeling content with yourself and where you are headed. Confidence comes from all of this and practicing skills in different areas of your life. Parenting can help or hinder these beliefs within our children, as can poor teaching at school.

There is growing realisation in the fields of emotional intelligence and mental health that living to very repetitive routines actually inhibits creativity, and therefore diminishes the ability to engage with one's environment and build meaningful relationships of true worth. Routines make us live out programmes and make us fall into the trap of living in our bodies rather than our minds. To quote Dr Joe Dispenza in his amazing book, *Becoming Supernatural*:

> If you keep doing the same routines over and over again, they will become a habit. A habit is a redundant set of automatic, unconscious thoughts, behaviours and emotions that you acquire through frequent repetition ... Over time you create a set of hard-wired neurological networks in the brain and you have emotionally conditioned your body to live in the past, and that past becomes your future.

It is a pretty depressing fact that so many people choose a lifestyle that will programme them into staying the same. I see the unschooling lifestyle as the tonic to this. We are creating all the time, and every day is different. Doing something new for the first time, produces new neurological learning – this shouldn't just be for the young!

We are living in a quickly changing environment, where the media and news coverage changes within seconds and we are constantly bombarded with information. Anxiety is at a reported high with teenagers suffering the most. In a time like this, to know yourself and feel confident in your worth is crucial for mental wellbeing.

Unschooling has been around since the 1970s, so there are many home-educated unschooler adults out in the world doing their thing. It happens and it works! Unschooling families are creating an environment of choice and responsibility, and this helps children grow into self-efficient individuals who can manage their own projects and enjoy their experiences. It comes down to trying and feeling and trusting. They do not have to live by the bell or the clock, and they get to find what makes them feel good and relish it as much as they want. They have parents that are conscious and praising them for their efforts, who show them love and affection as they grow up. All of this will build self-aware and confident adults.

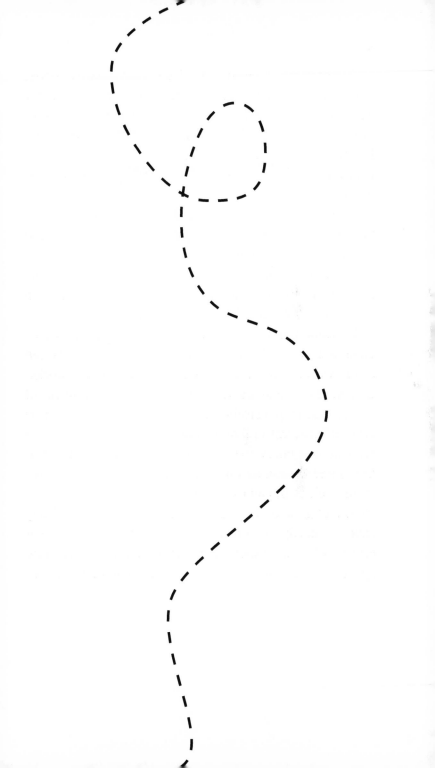

Live in the sunshine,
swim the sea,
drink the wild air.

Ralph Waldo Emerson

Chapter 6
Becoming Free

Deschooling yourself and your child is the most important focus you can have when you start home educating. To deschool is a kind of uncluttering of emotional baggage, setting down what you do not need and re-evaluating your life.

This valuable process might take time, depending on your experience at school. I have met families in the home education community who have had far more traumatic experiences than our own. Families where children have been relentlessly bullied and picked on by teachers, as well as other children. Sometimes, no help was offered to the parents and extreme stress and anxiety have caused physical illness. There may have been lack of sleep due to stress and depression, or mental health issues arising from the experience at school.

In these circumstances, the last thing your child needs you to do at home is set up a mini school. Even if this is done in love. Stop! You are the adult and it is now your responsibility to completely wrap your child up in love again, just as you did when they were a baby. The pillars of emotional strength need to be rebuilt and the way to do this is deschooling.

I remember reading about it at first and thinking, Yup, I'll do that, but in the back of my mind I planned to take it slow, not push too much. And that is not really deschooling. As time went on in our first few months it became apparent through my own behaviour and expectations that I had not properly deschooled myself.

I had found this amazing way to learn with my children and yet little anxieties crept to the surface now and again, like bursts of panic rising through all the fun and fantastic new experiences we were having. I would start thinking, 'but is this OK? ... can we learn while sitting in a field eating ice cream? ... maybe we need to do more book work ... we should practice writing more'. Or I would think about how they might be studying this or that at school now – did that mean we were behind? I realised that I needed to sit down with myself and really think hard about my own schooling and what my ideals and expectations were, at a deeper level.

In those early days, I kept thinking that we needed to sit at a table and do some pen stuff. That thought just kept coming up in my head over and over again. We were having a ball, learning was taking place all over the place, and yet I still had this little voice inside my head telling me it was not enough. When we did eventually sit down and they did five minutes of writing or using workbooks, I felt so happy that they were engaged and doing what looked like school. It was incongruent with what I knew was right for us as a family, which was unschooling, but the emotions were triggering me to think illogically.

Maybe you have these feelings and thoughts too. All of these questions are a natural process of your mind as it runs through the experience you are providing for your children, against your own memories of school and your beliefs about what learning should be. In deschooling, we allow these thoughts to come to the surface and answer the questions logically, and with reason. Try and take out the emotion, because that is your emotion, not your child's.

Subconscious conditioning

Our belief system (about who we are and what our experience has told us) is held in our subconscious. The subconscious is the part of the mind that does everything we do not need to consciously think about – it is creative, imaginative and holds all of our memories and emotional responses. All of our memories are neurologically wired into our brain and different experiences can trigger these neural pathways to experience the same feeling again and again. We then create patterns of feeling and thinking. This creates a subconscious program to live by. We actually program our brains through emotions, and can become addicted to the chemical released by those feelings. So much so, that when we try to change the behaviour or our perspective on a situation, we crave the chemical hit we previously got from the emotion.

When we live our lives without consciously thinking, we are using our conditioned memories and feelings to steer us through our experience. We are living within programmes that have been set up for us through conditioned thought and not rational thinking. This is fine for processes that do not need changing, but to look at things in a new light we require conscious thought, so we can upgrade our thinking through reasoning. When we step out of this perceived comfort zone (even if it is not comforting), like when we look at school in a new way, we need to rationalise these preconceived, programmed memories, the emotional reaction, and the physical feeling that they trigger.

Once we start to challenge the belief systems held in our deeper mind from childhood, this can trigger our emotions and alter our perception of our world. This is what happens when we are conditioned to think one way and we try to live against the conditioning. This is OK! This is a process, and it is natural. We are re-conditioning our brains to think something new, something better.

This is why deschooling is such an important and crucial step in becoming free of conditioning and emotional behaviour, to create a new outlook for our family that suits everyone's needs. It is tough at first to bring lots of thoughts up from your own experiences and rationalise them. All the while you are trying to keep everyone happy, juggle a business or a job and feed everyone! But it is a process that will happen, you just have to allow it to happen and be in the moment when it does – rather than act on those irrational thoughts. Do not start to pretend that you are a teacher, or try to impart your standards with emotional blackmail or by getting upset.

And remember, time is on your side, there is no rush. Especially if there has been trauma in your child's life. The best thing you can do at first is simply play. Go outside, build forts and rest. Your child needs to rebalance and so do you. The way to do this is to be together and get to know each other. Reconnect. If you feel guilt for having put them into school, know that it was not your fault. You were acting on conditioning, but you are awake now! Say sorry if it helps. Have a conversation with your child, however young, and allow them to see that you are a person forever learning too, just like them!

Listen to your child's ideas about how to learn: they know how they take in information best. For example, Rufus is an observer. He likes to watch and learn. Otis is a doer. He likes to get stuck in straightaway and find his own way with things. I am a reader, I like to learn concepts and theories from books and online guides and models then weigh them up in my mind. Jim is an auditory learner, he enjoys documentaries, music and debate. It's fun to think about how the whole family works together on this; each of you will have different ways of doing things and different strengths.

Confidence

As a remedial hypnotist I meet people who are struggling with identity issues such as low self-esteem, anxiety, lack of confidence or feelings of being not good enough. A lot of these feelings are held in the subconscious as beliefs of self, because they have been learnt in childhood. Anyone who has had a tough time in school will understand where these beliefs can start from. I do lots of important work with my clients to finally relieve them of this negative baggage that they are carrying around. One of the ways I help to change things is by using visualisation.

If lack of confidence is holding you back from truly going for it in this role as a home educator, a great place to start is to visualise yourself doing it as you wish to. Close your eyes and see yourself doing all the things you want to do. See your kids happily coming along and responding so well to their new normal and feel how you would feel knowing that this leap of faith was the right thing to do. Really go there, feel it in your body, see what you would see, hear what you would hear. Practice this a lot, and it will boost your confidence by upgrading your beliefs and emotions to fit the visualisation. Trust me this works, I do this all the time for myself and also coach others in doing so for many different reasons.

It works by engaging your subconscious mind and your autonomic nervous system into believing it is happening already. The autonomic nervous system is the part of our mind-body connection that we do not have to think about. It is the connection between our brain, spinal column and the parts of the body that determine chemical and hormonal balance. It is the primal system that helps us react quickly to perceived dangers and the intuitive system that creates good feelings.

This exercise can be done from a very young age. Before the age of about ten, we are fully subconscious, which means we do not use rational thought processes yet. We are fully in the present moment and react with feeling and emotion straightaway without any mindful analysis. This means that kids are amazing at visualisation because when they are young they are so adept at pretending, and using their imaginations to the fullest. Learning through play – which on another level is visualisation – is something that has taken place throughout our history since the dawn of time and should never be lost.

I would wholly suggest that you do some visualisation support with any child who has encountered a traumatic time at school, to help in the healing process that is deschooling. A point to make here is you only visualise a positive new reality, you do not look again at what happened, as that will further the trauma and will be detrimental to the process. New realities can be helped along with a positive outlook and new fun ways of living without trauma. Visualising themselves in a happy carefree environment will really help children get there quicker.

It has been proven that visualisation can alter not only perception in the mind, but it can also alter physicality too. In his incredible book *Psycho-Cybernetics*, Maxwell Maltz, the plastic surgeon turned psychologist, says 'Your nervous system cannot tell the difference between an imagined experience and a real experience. In either case, it reacts autonomically to information that you give it from your forebrain. Your nervous system reacts appropriately to what you think or imagine to be true'. This is important information, as it demonstrates how we can literally change our state of mind and heal from traumatic experiences through utilising imagination in the form of play and visualisation. Having this knowledge is powerful in itself.

Putting this into practice will enhance your personal growth and make you feel different on an emotional and physical level. When you feel run down, tired or anxious, sit for a moment and use visualisation to turn things around. Breathe deeply whilst doing this and you will enhance the experience and your energy.

You can do this with your kids too. If they are struggling with anything, get them to close their eyes and see themselves doing the thing easily. Guide them to feel great and powerful whilst they do it so easily and with a sense of relaxation and happiness and see how it changes their state away from anxiety. This works well in all sorts of situations, from lack of confidence about going to groups, to learning things like throwing or catching or hitting a ball. The brain uses memory all the time as a shortcut to knowledge, so by creating a new memory by visualising something, it upgrades to thinking you can do it already!

Confidence is something that is possible for all of us. It is negative belief that holds us back, not our inabilities. The belief that you are not good enough is not *your* belief. It has been put there by an event or another person and to let go of this belief is the most healing thing you can do for yourself and the next generation. After all, we are the parents, the guides to what is to come, so let's change the world by being the best people we can be, by letting go of beliefs that are not our own and forging forward creating a new positive outlook. And let's have confidence in the people we really are and want to become.

Our identity has a lot to do with this. Becoming a home educator may have shaken up your belief of who you are, but you are still a parent. You are not a teacher, and you should not try to be. Guide, certainly and loving parent definitely. But at the core of your being you are just you! And that is more than enough. Identity is something that changes all the time as we grow and experience new things in our lives. Think of the person you were ten years ago – I am sure that you are a very different person today. Time changes us. Experience changes us. Identity is a fluid and ever-changing thing. So embrace this insight and relax your grip on your personal identity because then you can really start living as the person you want to be.

This will help your children become who they want to be too. Letting go of traditional roles or hierarchies allows more freedom of expression and enables them to try to be who they wish to become. Allowing a higher level of freedom does allow for more expression whether through clothes, attitudes, hobbies or obsessions and the best thing to enhance their experiment in forging an identity is to stand back and let it happen – even if it is a bit cringeworthy sometimes! Rebellion is also something to look forward to because it is another way our children are expressing themselves.

Phases

As time goes by, you have to adapt. We all look back and remark how things change through time and how we are different people than we used to be, so we cannot expect the same situation to be the best for our kids forever. As your kids develop, things that worked before no longer will, and you will have to think on your toes, go through periods of adjustment and rebalance. I call it shifts, or phases.

As parents, we all know that remark don't we, 'it's just a phase' ... well it is. A phase of development. As the human brain and its millions of neural connections develop, we do go through a phase, let's call it a cloudy moment. On a neurological level, as the brain upgrades with new learning, the brain waves go from coherence, to chaos and incoherence, before settling back down once the new networks are uploaded to the system.

What this means from the outside is that children in certain phases might be more confrontational with their surroundings or their family for a while. A lot of parenting is about accepting and not reacting. Even though our own emotional balance is being tipped and pushed off the edge. Our kids know our buttons, of course they do, they are our buttons!

Our kids are here to help us learn about ourselves and develop our emotional intelligence. We can use these times to realise that we need to let go of emotional programming that we might still have running from the past.

There have often been times when my boys have been so rebellious and (in my perception) had an obvious obstinate and completely disobedient phase, only for one of them to go to someone's house and the parents have sung their praises when I picked them up, saying how wonderfully kind or polite they had been. Makes me think: It's just for me then! Even though it can be the most exhausting time, I am always on one level proud that my boys are strong in argument and strong enough to make a stand. We have to trust that our own behaviour and the way that we live out our days is being observed continuously and is being soaked up. I believe that the world needs more people able to express themselves freely and I hope my boys will be two men of the future who will stand up for their beliefs and morals.

Conscious Parenting

I want to talk a bit about conscious parenting here because I know first-hand how tricky this can be.

My Otis is what I call a spirited child. Some people, particularly if they have not had the pleasure of meeting him properly, may describe him as a wild child! He is a button-pusher for sure. He not only pushes my buttons, and his dad's buttons – he has the special ability to push the buttons of people he has only just met! He is an exceptionally confrontational person. So, being Otis's mum and protector and guide I have had to adapt my own comfort zone to include him and his confrontations with the world. What I have actually learnt is that he is a natural empath. He literally reacts to others' energy, he feels it, he has told me. Not everyone understands or believes this, but I see it.

Being a home educating mum does not mean you are more adjusting, or naturally able to not get fired up by your kids. Just because we choose to be with our broods every living moment, does not mean we have been given another set of skills with which to handle difficult times. The women I have met who home educate, are usually quite robust, outspoken, empathetic and kind. But we all struggle. Each and every one of us. We just do not give up, we take our responsibilities seriously, or we feel that we tried the other way and we got let down, so it is down to us now!

Wellbeing

Not only have I had to deal with my own mental wellbeing over the past few years but I have learned a thing or two about mindful wellbeing through my work. When you are a parent, home educating or not, you need to think about this. It is important. There are a lot of conditioned beliefs about parenthood that we all take on and use against ourselves as critical advice, which is not helpful or in any way healing. We have all heard of mother's guilt, the prescribed guilt that all mothers seem to accept. Guilt at the level of responsibility we have for taking decisions for our broods, weighed against the cost of our own life or what is best for us as an individual.

If we are to move on in this world we need to stop this cycle of hurt and self-criticism today! You are an expert on one subject in this world: You! You know when you are close to the edge, that edge of reason, rationality and emotional stability. Learn to see it coming and react before you go over that edge of the abyss. This is consciousness in action.

Hopefully you have a network of support around you that you can call on in times of exhaustion or stress or PMT. However, in case you do not, here are some tips to survive as a home-educating parent.

If the kids are smaller you might want to make a box of curios and things to do on their own. Get a big old plastic storage box from a hardware store, write the kid's name on and put it away for a 'cloudy' day. Fill it with things that are easy and safe to do and things they have not seen before that will keep them occupied for a while. When you feel like you are approaching that 'edge', get the box out and leave the room. Sit somewhere snuggly and breathe. Think positively about your life, look around and feel grateful, even if it is a mess. You are living the best life you can in this moment.

The emotion of gratitude has been shown to release chemicals that raise the functioning of the immune system. With the act of giving thanks, your body and brain believe its a time to feel good, and are triggered to heal and release endorphins to keep us calm and balanced.

Having an affirmation printed somewhere is helpful. I love quotes, and I have a few printed out around the house to remind me when I need extra encouragement, things like 'Raising boys is an honour and adventure!' or, 'Into the forest I go, to lose my mind and find my soul'.

Going into the forest – or just outside – is something that saves me every time. Just when I feel I cannot carry on anymore, we get shoes on, coats on and go outside. I have been known to run screaming and wailing like a Banshee up the garden and round in circles. They all probably think, Oh dear Mum's lost it again, but it clears my mind, it changes my state, it awakens my energy. Feel the cold air, the wind, the rain, and remember you are alive!

Also remember that you are never alone, because in the next town there is another home-ed mum or dad feeling just like you. Tired, frazzled, questioning why they chose the 'difficult option'. Luckily for us, we live in a time of easy communication. Get numbers and use apps to keep in contact and support each other. We are a tribe and a community, there are people here for you. And, it is not the difficult option, but that is something I have definitely felt from time to time. Doing the right thing does sometimes feel difficult, but to avoid the right thing is to remain in denial and that is not the way to change the world, or become conscious.

Another tip is to only take advice from other home educators, as they will understand better what you are going through. It is quite a unique circumstance and experience, and people who do not do it themselves, will not hand out the best advice.

Many things and experiences may get you to the edge sometimes: difficult behaviour, siblings fighting (this is usually the cause in my house). The best thing I ever came up with was 'Time Out' – my version. I go on a time out! I tell the boys, 'Mum needs a bit of quiet time' and I retreat to my bedroom or to my thinking bench at the end of the garden. Not for long, maybe with a cuppa, or to read a chapter of my book. Then I come back composed again, able to face the music once more. Conscious parenting is hard to do sometimes, but if you can bite your lip and see things through without losing your shit, you will make stronger human beings that respect you and themselves. And in the long run, that is worth everything.

I definitely clash with my boys when I am on my period. Fact. So a couple of years ago I decided it was not a bad idea to just not plan anything on those days. It is generally one or two days a month when I am particularly snappy or narky and this decision has relieved me of so much emotional pain and guilt. On those days we might watch films, walk the dogs or stay at home and I read my book while they play Lego or watch YouTube. We are still learning, but without the unnecessary guilt of attempting too much only to feel overwhelmed.

As home educators, we are actually in a good position to do mental wellbeing management, and what better example to hand down to our kids than to show that we know our limits and recognise when we need recuperation and rest. That is one of the best life lessons going.

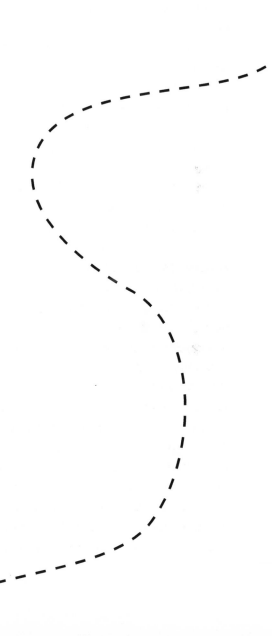

Blessed are the curious, for they shall have adventures.

Lovelle Drachman

Chapter 7
When to Go With the Flow

So nearly four years in, I heard the dreaded sentence come from Rufus's mouth. 'I want to give school another try'. I mean, what? why? how? ... Why? I felt all these questions splashing into my stomach. I went quiet and possibly quite pale. Then we got real.

Jim and I had discussed the possibility of either of the boys asking to try school again at some point. Apart from friends and cousins talking about it, the only exposure they have to school is in films. Films tend to portray schools as places to hang out with other kids, play sports and meet girls. Even Hogwarts has that going for it. I think Rufus felt like his negative experience happened a lifetime ago, and these representations of school seemed appealing. It was something he wanted to try again, or at least a way to get away from me for a while.

As Ru gets older I see him experimenting with his identity and I think home education seemed too co-dependent for him. He was looking for more independence, some time to perhaps test himself in a different environment on his own. I got it. I did not like it one bit, but I kind of understood.

Throughout that summer, there was a lot of talk about secondary school. Rufus's older cousin was starting at secondary and very excited about it, and his best mate was sitting his eleven-plus (an exam which ten-year olds take in some areas of the UK which still have a selective education system divided into 'grammar' and 'comprehensive' schools).

Ru was engaged in these conversations and probably saw his own home education as lacking prominent markers of age or steps in development, like moving to secondary school or exams to pass or fail. We know this to be one of the best things home education offers our children. Life can roll on without tests or huge upheavals, but I wonder if he felt somewhat left out. So we had a few in-depth conversations about the process of returning to school and what it would entail, and he still wanted to pursue it.

Once again I found myself in a school office, with Ru by my side, waiting to speak to the Head Teacher. It was a different school from before, one where we knew a few families and was relatively close to our home. I wanted Rufus to be in the meeting so he could hear everything that was said, after all it was his decision and his experience.

When the Head asked why he wanted to go back into the school system, Ru replied, 'I want to try it again'. The teacher did not look convinced and looked to me for support, but I must have convinced him even less because I was told that we should all encourage Ru to come to school on days that he might not want to. I nodded, but

I knew there was no way I was going down that route again!

They offered Rufus a place and he started the following week. We gathered some uniform, a nondescript black bag and a pair of smart black shoes from the local supermarket and off he went. He had no worries, a bit of trepidation and excitement, but a steely determination on his face that told me he was owning this experience, this was all his. I drove him to school, walked next to him to the entrance and said goodbye, all the time feeling sick and weird inside. I was feeling the anxiety and the worry. I actually felt quite tearful when I lost him through those doors.

I sat in the car for a moment before turning the key and asked myself why I felt like this. The answer that bubbled up was 'because it feels wrong'. Rufus enjoyed that first day, in fact he enjoyed the first week. After the second week he had found a love for maths lessons and enjoyed the competitive nature of the class, but he struggled in literacy. He was not much amused by the church service for Harvest Festival, and announced at dinner time that he reckoned most of the teachers were pretending to believe in God just to keep it going.

What was interesting to me and Jim was other people's reactions to Ru trying school again. Our next-door neighbour, a lovely lady in her seventies, flung her arms round him and told him how clever he was! One of Ru's aunties was so excited at the prospect that she insisted he look smart and gave him a new school haircut. They seemed to think we had woken up from our illness and seen the light.

It was obvious that their doubts about home educating

came from it not being the 'normal' thing to do. They do care for us, and they want the boys to do well, so they were relieved when it looked like we were doing the normal thing again.

To me though, it felt like we were conforming to something less real, less whole and too contrived. At the end of week three he got a week off. Half term. Oh what a relief! Ru was home and life felt normal again. We all got to hang out together and with our home-ed friends, to whom Rufus told stories of school days.

He seemed determined to go back right up until the Monday morning. Then, 'I don't want to go in Mum'. I asked, 'Today? Or ever?' 'Ever.' he said. I felt the tension starting to defrost from my shoulders. We sat down with Jim and weighed it up. We were fine with him coming out, but I wanted to make sure he had got his helping of whatever it was he had gone for. Ru decided he had experienced enough and wanted to choose home-ed.

He wrote a little letter of thanks to his teacher and the Head, and I drove down to the school to tell them the good news. They had been nothing but kind and supportive and I wanted to personally thank them. As I shook his hand, the Head had a look on his face like his expectations had been fulfilled. The secretary just did not understand, and although she was kind, she looked at me with puzzlement as I walked out the doors. I walked taller, and I could not stop smiling, one of those smiles that makes you feel silly because you just cannot stop it.

This emotionally moving experience completely cemented the fact that I believe in home education. I really believe. This experience was genuinely magnificent on many levels and, it seems now, was so necessary and well-timed. Ru had his chance to own the decision to go back into the school system and come out again. How empowering that must have been, to walk in there on his own and fall into line, only to weigh it all up and make a big decision to walk back out again. He has the benefit of knowing both options, knowing both worlds which seem so far apart from each other.

The sense of an 'all or nothing' decision around school did make me think about the system. Why could the school week not be more flexible, offering different start times or shorter weeks? But it is not my job to fix the problems, I am far too busy living away from that world and I am very happy living outside the box.

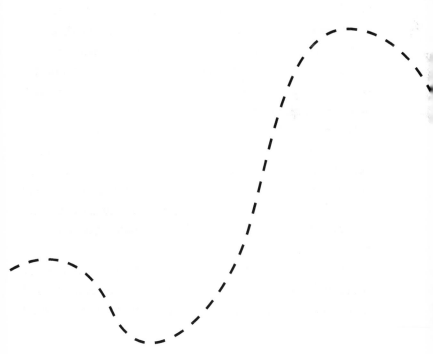

Try to learn to be, and see learning in all kinds of things.

Sandra Dodd

Chapter 8
Learning in Action

As home educators, how we learn is up to us. To quote the law in England once more,

> The parent of every child of compulsory school age shall cause him to receive efficient full-time education suitable –
> (a) to his age, ability and aptitude, and
> (b) to any special educational needs he may have, either by regular attendance at school or otherwise.

The words 'efficient' and 'suitable' are not defined; they are left to our own interpretation.

There is currently a government consultation into the registration of kids in home education, and as the number of home educated children in the UK increases, we are likely to get more 'official attention'. So it is a good idea to stay up-to-date with the latest laws and guidelines.

At present though, the situation is this. Our Local Education Authority requires us to write down an 'education philosophy', basically outlining what we plan on doing to educate our children. This is the document that they then use to weigh up whether you are doing what you said you would do. If they have serious concerns about the welfare and education of a child, LEAs do have the authority to issue a School Attendance Order.

Education philosophy

There is sometimes paranoia and anxiety around creating an education philosophy but there really needn't be. As long as you think about what education you want for your children and why, then it will be deemed suitable for your family. The day Jim and I found out I was pregnant with Rufus we started our education philosophy, we just did not label it that way. Whenever you have considered what is best for your child personally, you are contributing to your education philosophy. You just need to write it down.

The best way to start is by making a list. A list of all the qualities and skills you want for your child of the future. Mine included things like a knowledge of mental health, nutrition and how to cook, an understanding of the natural world and the seasonal changes, how to survive in the wild, a knowledge of geography and experience of different cultures, enjoyment of music, art, craftsmanship and ability to know themselves and understand how their mind and bodies work best.

This list sparks thoughts and plans about how to impart this through education, and they comprise your education philosophy. What you consider important, and how you are going to achieve it. You do not need to make it any more detailed than that. This is what you deem suitable and efficient for your family and it is what you can be held accountable to by your Local Education Authority. As long as you have thought it through and are showing signs that you are acting upon your method, it's all good. I get a call about once a year from the LEA; the officer asks some questions about what the boys have been doing, whether they are happy, etc. There is minimal contact and we have never met them.

Every LEA has its own set of practices and requirements, and things do change, so please do not take my word for it – look carefully at your own local government websites and check the latest documents.

Learning all the time

We have tried many ways to spark learning and inspire interest. A good one to start with is writing out a list of topics as a family, including anything that anyone wants to learn about. Then cut out all the topics and put them in a 'Topics Jar', for any time the kids get bored or do not know what to do. Picking topics from the jar at random keeps it interesting and spontaneous, but the kids have already had a say on them, and the subjects hold interest for them. What you do with these topics is up to you – some have turned into full-on projects or trips out, others have inspired collages and papier-mâché models and others have just been a subject to explore on YouTube. The best thing to do is roll with it. Each day is different and takes another turn along the journey of discovery.

'Strewing' is an amazing, under-the-radar way of leaving educational things around the house where the kids may find them. New books left on the sofa, colouring books or new pens on the chair in the kitchen, a magazine left on their bed, with no pressure attached, just strewn there. Then wait. It might produce excitement and fun times that day, or just get swept up in a pile and brought back out in two months' time. Either way, no pressure.

Another thing I have always done is found educational pictures, diagrams, or words, laminated them, and stuck them up in the kitchen and the bathroom. For months we had the name Charles Darwin just randomly stuck above the loo! It was there for Rufus to remember his name as he had Charles Dickens stuck in his head, but many guests commented on it. This worked a treat and he now knows and probably will never forget the difference between those two Victorian men!

We have had so many laminated things up around the house over the years. Currently in the loo we have diagrams of the water cycle and the human skeleton! One of my very good and trusted friends once said to me that 'a massive part of learning takes place as observation'. I hope she is right, as I do like a laminated print-out. I find they spark conversations within the family and when people visit, and at those times I get to hear the boys' explanations and see what has been retained.

I never test my kids' knowledge verbally or otherwise. I have always detested it when parents get their children to perform for others, like they have been trained to show off. It is not my way. I much prefer listening to them explain things to others in their own language, their own way and whether it is an elaborate version or a synopsis, this enables me to see how they have understood what we have researched and discussed.

Both my kids learn things over time, so will remark on subjects again and again in different ways over an extended period. Certain subjects that they have enjoyed or are particularly curious about will come up again and again and we will do everything we can to encourage more of this. As time goes by you develop an ear for subjects, and then you can keep a note and plan projects or day-trips or even holidays around these fascinating subjects or obsessions.

I love obsessions. I think 'obsession' is a dirty word in our society but wrongly so. To have an obsession in life is to have a passion. An overwhelming passion and drive to want to experience something deeply, I can only see this as a good thing. After all, most of the world's top sportsmen and women have only got to the top of their game by obsessing over their chosen sport. Scientific breakthroughs come from obsessive research and experimentation. Incredible artworks develop out of obsessions with ideas or materials.

We have had a few obsessions in our house. Each time one arises I do my utmost to help the obsession flow by providing relevant material. This could involve a trip to the library to take out as many books on the subject as we are allowed, finding videos, diagrams and paintings online, doing colouring pages, discovering places to visit, watching films, theatre productions or TV shows, meeting real people who know about the subject, or eating related food – anything that resonates and encourages the passion!

The story of the Titanic is one that has come around again and again and we are planning to go to Ireland next year to see the museum. We have built the Lego model, watched the film a few times, YouTubed the conspiracy theories, made a papier-mâché model, added up the death-toll and talked all about class systems and all sorts, based on Otis's obsession. During the Dr Who obsession we discussed alien life, parallel universes, magic, time-travel – so many deep subjects because of that one! We also embarked on a trip to Wales one weekend to see the Dr Who collection and experience Cardiff. Planning a trip is a learning experience in itself, the kids are part of the planning when we travel, so they get to see how it is done and make decisions about the itinerary.

Volcanos, bikes (motor, balance and mountain), the solar system, earthquakes and tsunamis, submarines, dogs, mud, Ancient Egypt, metal music, Lego, and Xbox are all obsessions that have come and gone, often to come back round again later. We all have our outlets of passion and curiosity and as long as we are all looking for something we are learning too. I have tried many ways of getting educational content into our home and sparking interest but the main point that I have learnt again and again is that the more pressure you put onto learning, the more rebellion you will receive! Believe me!

When I have had time, I have enjoyed setting up tables in the evenings, so they looked inviting and interesting for the boys in the morning. This really worked when they were smaller. The technique is inspired by the Reggio Emilia method, developed by Loris Malaguzzi. His idea to create arrangements of objects as 'provocations' which would invite children to be inspired and curious appealed to my artist's mind and Rufus's observing way. I would gather flowers and natural found objects such as conkers, weird sticks, whatever was in season, and present them on a table beautifully laid out, with some paper, paint, play dough or clay. But I would not pressure them to do anything, they would just set about experimenting and finding out what to do themselves. It is supposed to be student-centred and self-directed, and I saw it as a form of beautiful, extreme strewing!

I did a lot of imaginary play with my boys too. When we played vets I would incorporate weighing the stuffed toys, writing their names on a big white board, categorising animals into types, making pretend foods and getting the boys to divide it up equally amongst our 'poorly' animals. We would play doctors and I printed off X-ray images from a home education freebie-download site and used my light box to figure out what was what. I would be bandaged and given sugar-water medicines. We would play chefs and make real food, laying the kitchen table out as our restaurant with name cards and menus all made by the boys. This list is endless and the only limit is your imagination.

If you are reading this and thinking that you are not imaginative, take it from me, you are. You just have to let go of the uptight adult and find that inner child again. The more you get into the role, the more the kids will accept it and the more they learn – so there is your reason to be a bit silly and play!

Natural learning, or spending time outside is recognised as hugely beneficial for sensory development. This benefit is being lost in our ever more sterile environments. I personally love the outdoors and always take my boys outside in the fresh air. When they were little this was never an issue, and we have acquired many different sand pits, mud kitchens and different play equipment over the years. As tinies, they always had their shoes off and got fully immersed in outdoor play. This has definitely set up a memory bank within both of them and even though they love gaming and watching films, they have a natural call to the outdoors. Although sometimes I have to push a bit these days to get them out the door, as soon as they are out they love it once more.

My own love of the wild outdoors comes from a memory bank within me of regular trips to Scotland as a small child, and because of this I draw happiness and balance from being outside in nature. I want my boys to have a grounding in the outside too, so whatever they do in their adult lives, nature will provide them relief and solace when they need it.

A daily walk can provide much learning and sensory development and many conversations will be sparked along the way. Get a bit of tree-climbing or river-wading in too, and it will turn into an adventure. Being outdoors regularly also gives us all a greater understanding of time,as nature intended, with seasonal changes and subtle nuances that can be visibly measured, experienced and discussed. An understanding of how nature works and continues to thrive throughout the seasons is evident from the shortest of walks if one is able to get into the present and open the senses to the experience.

Trying different groups is a fabulous way to gain support and inspiration and sometimes even a bit of time off as the kids play together. Most home education social groups do not have a minimum sign-up period. If there is,

I would suggest staying clear in the early days. There are plenty of one-off sessions or drop-in groups to try before you commit.

Experiment with rocking up at different times. Sometimes it is good to get there a bit early and allow the group to build up around you, especially if the kids (or you) have some social anxiety. Or, it can be good to turn up a bit late, so the kids already there are warmed up and ready to meet a new friend. Set up the feeling in your family that there is nothing to lose. Do not lay down expectations of making new friends, or having to go back, or pressure of any sort.

I really down-played groups at first because I knew Rufus was anxious, he always hated parties and things like that. So I would say we were just going to pop in for ten minutes. Often we would end up staying for the whole thing, sometimes we would bail after thirty minutes, but that was fine. Again, I would not put any pressure on them. If they did not like the group's dynamic, I would just say, 'Oh well, what shall we do now? Go to the park for a bit?'

We have always used car journeys as a time to reflect and debate and learn. I have an old Land Rover that I purchased from a guy in a car park one summer evening. It was all legit, but it did feel a bit dodgy! Well, I love this car, it is a bit of a heap but it was cheap and she still goes, everything fits in just about and I am not precious about it. With two boys, many small dogs and an outdoor lifestyle this car fits for now. When I bought the car the radio did not work. At first we were sad not to have any car tunes, but we soon adapted and forgot what it was like to have any noise other than the engine. After four years, I finally got a new radio fitted this summer. It was strange to have the radio back and very often the boys opt to turn it off so we can chat.

We do a lot of questioning and observing from our car. We once got stopped in the road just a few miles from our house, coming back from a home-ed group. An air ambulance hovered then landed right in front of us, and we saw people being stretchered out of cars into it and away they went. We saw tow-trucks and police doing their job, as if it was some macabre theatre production playing out in front of us. What a learning event for us all, and it sparked conversations about a myriad of things that went on for days. Another time on the way back from the beach, before the school holiday hoards descended, we saw a lorry with a trailer of hay completely on fire.

Now, I am not suggesting you drive around looking for disasters to observe, but merely remarking how we get out and about a lot more than most kids, so we get to see and experience a lot more real happenings. We learn from so many potential sequences of events and it is amazing.

I really want to emphasise that home educating with confidence is about living a whole life, a life that is geared towards curiosity at every turn, not only for your children but for yourself. When you stop thinking about education as something that you have *to do*, and realise that it is naturally occurring and can be achieved while living, you will gain a deeper satisfaction in general and start enjoying the process and thus gain confidence. Shutting out negativity and conditioning takes time and failing one day is learning something the next. And the fabulous thing is – we have time on our side.

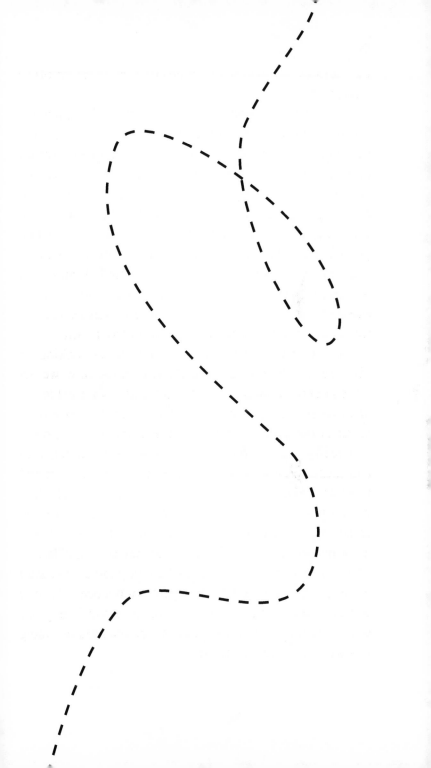

*Inhale confidence,
exhale doubt.*

Chapter 9
Possible Side-effects

Unschooling is a holistic way of life, and soon becomes so natural and fluid it is a new normality. What are the possible side effects of this new normal? Well, in my own experience there have been a few.

My children are more determined, opinionated, and sure of their own authority. Both my boys are now self-confident and feel they have a right to voice their opinion and be heard. This has always stood in my house – even as tinies I would allow them to butt-in to conversations and I would listen to them over the adult. This displeased some adults, but I did it for a good reason.

Children live in the moment. They cannot hold onto their thoughts the same way adults can. Until a child is nearing ten they are fully subconscious and their rational mind is yet to fully develop, so therefore they live in a very immediate frame of mind. To make them wait until the adults have stopped talking, is to miss an opportunity to hear your child's view and this is something I am not prepared to do. However, unschooling has taken this to a new level.

My boys are very vocal and have very strong viewpoints. They are also rebellious and cheeky. So all in all they can be a controversial presence in a 'normal' setting! This can have the side-effect of embarrassment for me, but it is something I have had to get over and learn to be proud of. At the end of the day, they are experimenting with who they are and what they believe in. It is interesting that children voicing their opinion is still seen as unusual in our society.

One major side-effect of home educating from a very young age, as with Otis who never attended school, is that the children do not have the usual timidity or deference to adults. Otis is famous for saying his mind to whoever he is speaking to, whether they be ten or sixty! At first I would cringe, but after re-thinking my conditioning on this, I am actually immensely proud. He thinks of himself already as just as important as anyone else. He has this self-belief because he has not been dismissed or belittled (apart from by his brother of course!). He chats away with anyone, whether it be to an old lady in the haberdashery shop about diabetes and free range eggs, or a man on a train about crocodiles. These conversations and acquaintances are completely his, I am never involved. He holds his own and always has since he was very small.

We allow swearing in our house too, apart from at each other. This is something that obviously divides opinion too. I found that although there was a period of a lot of swearing in and out of the house, it has settled down to a level that is OK to me. It is not a rebellious act to swear in front of us, so it is not so fun! I have always told the boys that swearing constantly will only undermine them, as people will assume they do not know many words and they will be misjudged as stupid.

On the subject of vocabulary, I have always used words with my boys that might be considered too advanced for little kids, as my own mum did with me and my sisters. I like language and finding out where words come from, so I will use as varied a vocabulary as possible. I have never dumbed it down for my kids!

There is a lot of confrontation in our house, due to my boys' boisterous nature. This would probably be the same even if they were at school. But because they are at home together a lot, they do have a great bond, which is not differentiated by being in different year-groups or grades. This means they see themselves as equal, and they battle it out for superiority and the final say in many situations. Because we are together most of the time this can be quite exhausting, and is one of the things I admit I find tough to deal with. This is my issue and I am striving to let go of my emotional responses. I tell myself that it is a phase, but I am not so sure. There are times when it seems better or worse, and time will tell how it evens out and how it will affect them both.

We make sure they have some time apart, as it does us all good to be separate for a while. Ru and Jim go mountain-biking together and Otis likes to go and stay at his uncle's house with his cousins. To rebalance I walk my dogs, which is my haven, and I throw in as much time on my yoga mat as I can, but still get interrupted sometimes. I remind myself that very soon my children will not need me in the same way and I will probably miss it.

A great positive side-effect to unschooling is the slowing of time. I mean, our perception changes. When you have a handful of appointments per week instead of per day, time goes slower. On the whole, we can eat when we are hungry and exist in a more open time-frame. In fact, I try not to look at the clock too much, especially if we are having a day at home. I try to follow a natural rhythm rather than a clock face. Children do this naturally anyway. Living slower is quite a rebellious act in itself, and is taking off around the globe as a recuperating and healthy way to live.

We rest when we need to, and eat more healthily too because we are not in a rush. We like to cook and bake and we have veggie boxes and recipe boxes delivered, and I see the boys tasting and trying new things. I have allowed them to cook since they were tiny and both of them know quite a few dishes. Because we know where they are in their development, we can trust them with sharp knives and kitchen utensils. We are able to coach them in skills and facilitate experiences because they are with us so much.

Unsurprisingly, we are healthier. I cannot remember the last day either of my kids was ill. We get the odd runny nose, and germs must go around, but not in the same way as at school. Because we are less stressed, and are aware of emotions rather than repressing them for hours in a school room, we deal with our feelings, and our immune systems are less compromised.

Another side-effect of unschooling is the sense of freedom that comes from the outdoors. For me this is one of the top bonuses of home education. My kids and I are not contained inside. It seems silly to me that most of the UK's school-age children are kept inside for most of their waking day. If I were to stay inside for that long every week without getting a long walk or tinkering in the garden or sitting on my thinking chair in the sun I would go quite mad.

I take it for granted now that I get to go outside whenever I feel like it. My boys are not afraid of dirt, or wet or cold. On the contrary, the more extreme the weather the more excited they get. They cannot resist any open water and have been known to get in a river in November! Otis is crazy for running around in the rain and rolling in mud. Even though he is nearly seven, he cannot resist it. Needless to say, I always have towels and spare clothes in the boot of the car.

I love home education for keeping my kids connected to nature and feeling at home outdoors. When I see other children so clean and orderly, scared to get dirty shoes, I feel a sadness for Mother Nature who is losing so many souls to the inside world of sterility and allergies.

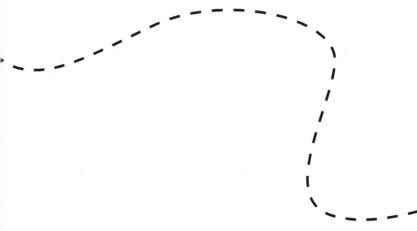

Imagination is more important than knowledge. For knowledge is limited.

Albert Einstein

Chapter 10
Balance and Rebalance

Sleep

Sleep is the most important job of the day. I remember when I first heard my hypnotism trainer and mentor say this. I thought, really? Surely sleep is a little bit over-rated? I had functioned for years without a good eight hours in the sack. Both my boys were light and broken sleepers as babies, and I had adapted to their routines. I had one that woke up regularly throughout the night and then the other who woke up bright and early with the sun... in the summer! I was a zombie-mummy for a few years, but still held down my part-time career and co-ran a business from home. When I look back at those early days of parenting I do not know how I did it.

Co-sleeping was something we did from the beginning. It just made sense for us to all sleep in one room rather than repeatedly try and put the kids back in their own rooms when they came to be closer to us. It worked, and although Otis still woke up through the night, we would get back to sleep quicker if we were in the same bed. I advocate co-sleeping to any family who struggles with sleep. The priority is for everyone to get some good deep sleep, so do whatever it takes for that to happen.

We were still co-sleeping when we moved into our current house, and we decided to buy the biggest mattress we could find and make our own bed from pallets. That way we could all fit in and have enough room to be comfortable too. Nowadays it depends on our day as to where the kids sleep. The sofa becomes a bed if we are watching a film together and one or both of them fall asleep. This is fine, because our agenda is to get good sleep for everyone.

Not trying to control the process lessens the stress. We do not have set bedtimes for the boys, which would need policing or enforcing. However, we do have an awareness of what sleep the boys individually need, and will set up the wind-down time in the house depending on the week's events or goings on. Time is not a rule to live by in our house after all.

Do not get me wrong, we have been up and down with this, but whenever we all get tired and the kids refuse to get ready or brush their teeth, it is because of pressure and stress. I then remember what the agenda is, and we all calm down. We cuddle and snuggle. We put lavender in the oil burner and something quiet and calming on the TV like David Attenborough's smooth tones or Bob Ross's friendly voice, and we all stop stressing.

Turning off

There is something else I have had to learn to do: turn off.

I used to get the boys to sleep, wherever they were, then I frantically caught up with emails and social media late into the night. I was trying to fit everything in, and one option was to divide my attention, into daytime with the kids and evenings to work. It turns out it is not the best option.

Staying up late on phones and screens disturbs our production of melatonin, the hormone that regulates sleep. For better sleep we need to switch the screens off, turn down the lighting and create an environment to begin relaxation. Since taking this seriously, my sleep has drastically improved. I turn the screens off around 10.30pm and try to be aware of what I am doing with my time before bed, rather than losing hours to social media.

Relaxation

I have not always been good at finding time for relaxation. I always seem so busy, and the feeling of not having enough time can be overwhelming. However, in my professional life I preach to my clients about how important it is to relieve stress and anxiety. Realising this, and that I have to lead by example after all, I have started to implement relaxation into my days.

I see any process that helps me become more focused and less stressed, or that retunes my energy, as rebalancing. It is detoxing from stress hormones or feelings of being overwhelmed that may build up over time through the consistent demands of home education. Red wine sometimes helps too!

You will know what is best for you, but ideally have a few things that you do just for yourself and incorporate movement, stillness and focus. I love walking my dogs on my own. We take them out a few times a week with the boys, but I make sure to grab some time on my own in the mornings before Jim leaves for work, and in the summer evenings. I find this really rebalances my mind and makes me feel so good.

I have recently discovered meditation, and am finding time for it by getting up earlier. Each morning I follow a guided meditation through headphones, while sitting in a chair in the lounge. This helps me to start every day fresh and without emotional baggage; it has really awakened something in me and has upped my natural energy.

Yoga is a form of movement that I love to do and I create time for. It is the most amazing thing for tension and a fuzzy head. I used to go to a class but I found it difficult to commit each week, so now I use online yoga videos. It is free and I can fit it into my day, which works for me. I would recommend this to everyone.

Eating well is essential for health and energy levels – and is another thing that I learnt the hard way. I used to take time to sort out my children's diet and mine would take a grab-and-go approach. I love cooking, but when it 'eats' into time which could be spent working, I tend to take the less holistic approach. But recently I have been told that I'm anaemic, and this has taught me that I need to focus on my nutrition to be the best I can be. Taking care of yourself is absolutely paramount for feeling the best you can. If you find yourself feeling drained or stressed, have a look at your nutrient balance and double check it is in order, as I have had to do. After all, you play a pivotal role in the home educating lifestyle, and to be on form consistently you need to take care of yourself!

Do not be afraid to ask for help or support. Help getting a specific job done or a loving hug both go a long way when you are not feeling your best. It is not weakness to know your limits; it actually takes immense strength to know when to stop.

Grabbing bits of time to yourself, when you can, is key to staying sane! In fact, alone-time itself is a luxury when you home educate. I did not foresee that initially, but it can be quite intense. Often, after a crafting hour, or after coming in from a walk or a group event, I say, 'Right! Mum needs some quiet time so go and do what you want'. My boys love gaming so they will happily go and play in their rooms. I can then have a cuppa or read for a while, or do something to relax and rebalance. A good soak in the bath with some essential oils and a book is a luxury I get to enjoy once in a while that allows me to be completely alone.

Trying to be mindful and in the present is a great habit to pick up. If the boys are playing outside I will do a spot of gardening or clearing the garden. 'Pottering' I think the term is. I want to be mindful and present, but not necessarily always with the boys and in their personal space.

Steve Biddulph makes a great point in his book *More Secrets to Happy Children*: 'Many people have lost the knack of just being, they think they are wasting time or not achieving if a day just drifts by. Yet if you want to get through to your kids then you have to get yourself back into present time'. He also says that 'happiness, like a child, dwells in the present'. One of my favourite things about being a home educating family is that family time is pretty much all the time – we do not need to worry about having so-called 'quality time', but live mindfully and present together.

Work

The topic of work follows the subject of rest, because to even entertain the idea of working, we must be getting good 'down time' too. Jim and I have run our business for nearly twenty years, and through that time our life has changed rather a lot. We have been on a learning curve, figuring out how to balance and shape our lives whilst running a business and this is something that we still work on today.

We both adore being in the driving seat of our lives. But with self-employment comes the huge responsibility for our own family and income, but also that of staff members too. It is a constant juggling act and one that can never be taken for granted – we have to continually re-evaluate what we want out of life and discuss openly how to achieve it.

I love what we do; it is creative and feels worthwhile. It is also very time consuming, and if allowed to, it can eat into our family life. In fact, it is pretty impossible for the two worlds to be separate and I am OK with this. When I was growing up, my parents had a business together and at times it seemed like the business was the baby who took the most attention. But living in this environment as a kid I learnt lots about what worked and some of what did not. I try to involve the kids in our careers, so they understand what we are doing and why, and they do not see it as taking us away from them, but rather providing for us as a whole. I hope that they can also see the value in working hard but at the same time enjoying what you do.

A few years ago I started my new Hypnotattoo and therapy venture, and I had to study. This added another ball to juggle, but I so wanted to do it and felt so passionate about what I was learning, that somehow I made it happen. I am glad I did. As the boys start to become young men I too am growing and developing, showing them that I am always learning and putting into practice what we preach to them.

So how to fit it in? It has been said that we work best in ninety minute to two hour stints, and working flexibly in this way works for me. I am far more productive knowing I have two hours set aside, rather than cramming work into my evenings. I have re-jigged my approach so I get chunks of time during the day. This is easier now that my boys are a bit older and have their own interests, but I think I could have managed my time better before if I had thought it through more.

Flexible working goes hand in hand with home education. I believe flexible working hours are the way forward across the board, and as time goes by they will become more normalised. The need for people to be in the office will become redundant as more people work from home, using technology to shake up the working week and work more productively around the family. It just makes sense.

This is how I do it: I short-cut things using apps, I shoot my Facebook videos for my therapy business while walking the dogs and I delegate some jobs to others online. I make lots of lists in notebooks all over the place as my mind is always whirring with ideas. I see clients at set times and days, and use the two hour stints to study, write blogs or case notes and draw tattoo designs.

Using technology to work flexibly is a great way to run a business or part of a business from home. As Emma Gannon says in her book *The Multi-Hyphen Method*,

> Technology has allowed us to rebel against what has been the norm for so many years. It has given us more freedom than we ever dreamed of. We can change our set parameters of the working day, use tools and machinery to tick off items on our work to-do list and communicate with others around the world with a click of a button … We've seen the demise of the job economy and the rise of the freelance economy.

This is great for the home educating community. Nowadays we can run a business from our kitchen table, become an Instagram sensation and have our kids around while we do it.

As the nature of work changes globally, home education becomes a more logical choice. If we are able to make money and support ourselves from home, does it not make the school system a little bit obsolete? Home education makes sense in this age of increasing technology, when we can learn online, pass exams online and live to our own schedules, balancing our own time and projects to make time to relax and explore the world.

The age of the nine-to-five job, or a lengthy career that spans a lifetime is over. There is a choice between being sucked into long days and long commutes, never being off duty from a precarious job; or making our own lives as we want them to be. The changing world of work effects not just parents who want to home educate now, but more significantly, the children who we are guiding to become independent adults. Our kids will need a skill set that stands out from the crowd, and confidence in who they are if they are to make it in this new era. I have no faith that the archaic school system is preparing its students at the speed which is necessary to keep up with changing technology.

I can envision a school system with flexible hours, a holistic approach to mental health and wellbeing, and daily outdoor sensory experiences. It would have more creative and vocational courses beginning at primary age, and a community-led, group-learning experience at its base. Idealistic as this sounds, I do believe it is what we need to move forward as a society. Though I do not see it happening any time soon.

On the other hand, I am excited about how radical parenting is right now creating a home education movement in this country. So many people have had enough of an obsolete system, and are taking responsibility to make changes happen. This is epic, and will change our country's future for the better. If we continue with confidence and conscious thinking, we could even change the world!

Never help a child with a task at which he feels he can succeed.

Maria Montessori

Chapter 11
Conscious Praising

Conscious praising is something that Jim and I try to do, and it started quite naturally for us. As the boys got a bit older it became apparent that praise is a big subject in raising children. We realised that compared to others – when we were people-watching or around different parents in different situations – we praised slightly differently from the majority.

For example, at a playground we would allow our boys (no matter what age they were) to scale whatever they felt like at whatever height, and explore openly. We did not hover, we stood back and watched how they were doing things and if we felt they needed guidance, because they got frustrated or stuck, we would guide them with words and encouragement on how to get out of the situation or get up higher. We would be calm and reassuring but we would not praise them. Other parents in the same situation seemed to be coaching their children and saying things like, 'You're so clever, look at you! You are amazing at that!' We wondered if we were being too traditionally British – were we being hard on them by not succumbing to the cheerleader approach? But it just did not feel right to us to over-praise.

We observed how people spoke differently to their children, almost becoming like characters on children's TV, speaking louder and in a higher tone. I could not stand it. My boys have always been spoken to as people, even when they were babies. I have always just chatted to them like they are older. As tiny babies I may have been a bit squeakier to get them to look at me, or smile! But generally I treat them like I do other people. I am full of support and encouragement but not praise.

Conditional praise, unconditional love

Steve Biddulph, in his book *More Secrets to Happy Children*, talks about praise and how in his opinion there are two types of praise that children need: 'one kind is unconditional praise – this means we let them know "I love you because you are you". They don't have to earn this love and they can't ever lose it.' He says, 'imagine how good this feels – to be unconditionally loved, just because you exist'. He goes on, 'the second kind is conditional praise. This means that we tell them, "I appreciate your actions"… It's OK to tell your kids what you don't like as well – as long as you don't call them names.'

I can see the trend for over-praising on television, in films and when we are out and about with other parents. The media and real life versions influence and reinforce each other. I think it is part of a shift across generations. My parents' generation, who were born in the 1950s, were brought up in an old-fashioned way when children were not given much attention at all. Children were to be seen and not heard, and certainly not listened to. Physical punishment was typical at home and at school.

When that generation had children in the 1980s, they felt that they needed to remedy the parenting they had experienced themselves. Over time, parenting has had an overhaul and it has almost gone too far the other way. Nowadays, some parents – who want to do the right thing by their children – seem like cheerleaders, praising their kids if they do literally anything.

We can already see the consequences; children who were brought up with this over-praising mind-set have developed a lot of anxiety in their late teens and early twenties through to their adult years too. It does not enhance self-esteem in the long term to set down beliefs in someone that they are 'amazing' or 'really intelligent' or 'awesome'. In fact, it sets them up for a self-esteem crash in later years. As a remedial hypnotist, I often treat people who are suffering because of over-praise in their childhoods. They have perhaps been told how intelligent they are, how awesome they are. This has set up a belief in them that they are somehow extraordinary, and their ego is inflamed. This is not true self-belief which comes from their experiences, but is conditioned from outside. And then as young adults, the bubble pops and they feel quite ordinary and lost. I am not saying that praise should not be given, far from it, but I do think it should always be a conscious act. There needs to be a conscious thought process and knowledge of what you are praising.

For example, when a child is attempting something that is new and difficult, encouragement will help them persist at the struggle. Encouragement is being beside them while they battle it out, vocalising your support: 'I believe in you, you can do this', 'keep going'. Praise will not help, it will almost undermine the struggle and add to the frustration. If they are so awesome, how come they cannot achieve their goal instantly? When they struggle through and get the result they wanted, then praising them for persisting with the struggle will help them the next time they have to do something that is not easy. So here we are setting up a positive regard for struggling to achieve learning, and praise for the process rather than the outcome. The praise then builds them up but also builds momentum for the belief that when they persist, their reward is the achievement of the goal itself, not praise from an outside source. The goal becomes transferable, but the belief in the struggle and their abilities to overcome it become inherent. From tying their shoelaces, to balancing along a beam, to passing exams, to learning just about anything.

Praising future adults

There will come a day when our children need to self-motivate, and if the tank that holds belief in their achievements is full of praise for results, or empty praise that they are simply awesome, they will not truly believe in themselves and they will look for validation from outside. Having us there beside them, as home education allows, is sometimes all children need in order to develop a self-encouraging belief. Be there as a stable and secure source of communication and conscious encouragement, be authentic, and this will provide all that is necessary to build self-esteem.

Bragging about how amazing your child is at this and that, may make you feel great but it will be detrimental to your child. They have to build their own internal belief system and if they do not agree with what they hear, they will be full of self-doubt and over-deliberation as adults.

If they do believe the hype, they will have inflated beliefs and these will either get knocked out of them by others, or when the bubble finally pops, perhaps at university, in their job or their first relationship, it will bring a sense of sadness, confusion as to who they are and a feeling of depression. They might feel as though their whole life has been a lie, or develop a feeling of not fitting in. If they have been constantly told they are amazing or over-achieving, they may develop a belief that they are superior to others and this will give them unrest when they try to form relationships in their teenage years and early adulthood.

All of this boils down to how praise is handled by the caregivers in the child's life, and if it is done consciously with the future-adult in mind, then I am sure the caring parent will praise and encourage with confidence. This in turn will produce a belief system within the child that will serve a lifetime of authenticity. They will have the ability to learn new things, keep going, and believe they can achieve anything they put their minds to.

We have to elevate our own conscious thinking to parent successfully, and for home educators especially, this can seem never-ending and intense; a continual conscious process. As long as you remember that you are human and that you will make mistakes, and when you do, you have the decency to apologise to your partner and your children, then it is all good. In fact, it provides another lesson for your children that you too are still learning, as an adult.

You are
the expert on you.

Tim Box

Chapter 12
What Others Say

I remember during that first week of home educating, being out and about with the boys felt weird. The schools had gone back, and I realised there were no other kids about. I looked down the High Street and there were a few toddlers and pushchairs but it was obvious that mine were school age, and were not at school. I felt a bit strange, like I was doing something wrong.

Were people looking and thinking we were skiving, or from some religious cult? Were we being judged? It is a funny thing to go against the grain. You would think that I would be used to it by now – I do have bright pink hair and am covered in colourful tattoos – but this felt different. This was not about me, this was my kids being judged and I did not like that feeling.

To be honest, I don't know if anyone did look and judge us that day. It was probably my own paranoia because I was still assembling my own judgements about what we were doing. Anxiety is like that. Our perception of a threat invokes an emotional response, whether that threat is real or just perceived. The fight-or-flight hormone adrenaline is released whether it is actually happening or not. I felt a little anxious and I also felt very protective. Judgement from others can be a hard thing to deal with.

Handling the questions

When judgement comes from strangers, we can logically manage it. You basically have three choices: educate them, ignore them, or have some fun with it.

When the lady at the checkout asks your child, 'No school today?' you can tell her that you are home educators, and what that involves, like learning all the time, and how you think the future won't rely so much on grades, but on standing out as a person who knows themselves and how passions are better to follow rather than exam results, blah blah blah.

Oh believe me, I have been out and about lecturing my belief. In those early days, I felt I had to tell everyone who asked, or did not understand, all about what home-ed was, to me at least. Now I realise it was for my own benefit rather than theirs. I was airing my beliefs out loud so I could hear them, better manifest them and test them. As the checkout lady's eyes glaze over and you can see her thinking, I wish I hadn't asked, you realise most people do not care about unschooling or your family's educational philosophy, and you stop bothering so much!

So we started to give more fun and rebellious answers to the same old question we get asked all the bloody time. 'Not in school today boys?' they say in the bank, supermarket, cinema, car park, swimming baths, garage, anywhere you go... We started to come up with fun responses, such as 'No we don't do school' and then stare! Or, 'We don't believe in the school system', which is best said by the youngest member of the family to have the most impact. Or, 'School sucks!' That was definitely an Otis remark. I just nod and smile sweetly and get on with packing the shopping. We have given up trying to educate random people, because what is the point of that? I have made the best decision for my family at this time and I have more expertise about my family's needs than anyone who does not know us!

Personally, I have not had too much negativity from outsiders to our choices. This may be to do with what I look like and because I come across as fairly sure of myself. I look like someone who does not fit in, so it makes sense to people who do not know me that I would do something crazy like take my kids out of school.

But I have heard plenty of stories from good friends of mine, who are all amazing mums and home educators, about nasty comments, disbelief or negativity expressed in front of their kids. When this happens there is only one option. IGNORE THEM. They have no idea what you have been through, and the process of conscious, logical, rational debate you have had in your own mind. These people are resistant to change or thinking out the box; in fact people who are downright negative and rude to people about their personal choices should be put in a box! It never helps anything to be pessimistic and not open-minded about something just because it is different.

I would actually go as far to say that if you have a person like this in your life at the beginning of this process, it is probably best to shut them out for a while. Make some space for the sake of your mental well-being and your self-development, until a time comes when their opinion does not hurt you emotionally. Then they can come back in. If they are determined not to open their mind, you can ignore them some more.

Friends and family

Jim and I are a strong couple when it comes to outside influence. We tend not to get shaken by others' opinions because, on the whole, we agree with each other. So that forges a strength between us. Home educating on your own as a single parent, or within a relationship with someone who does not get the home education thing just yet, can be the toughest place to start from. But there is a host of support for you.

Every home educator who has been doing it for a while is confirmed and assured in their belief that this is a better way for them and their kids. I urge you to go and find these people and talk to them. They will happily boost your confidence, chat over anything you are struggling with, make you laugh and maybe cry with stories of what they have been through, and they will give you a hug if you ask too! Honestly, this community is one of the most supportive and open-minded group of random, intelligent and opinionated people, and it grows every day.

When negativity comes from a person that you otherwise respect, love and trust, it is very challenging. In our family, at times, I can see people sometimes think, Oh my, now they're going too far! Sometimes they do not understand how the hell this is all going to pan out, and they are worried for us. Or, they just think we are bonkers. (Though I suspect, considering other things we have done in our past together, they have come to that conclusion already!)

We have to remember how we are all conditioned. We hypnotists have a concept called the Map of Reality. Everybody's map is unique to them, and develops throughout their life as they collect experiences. Some of the fundamental beliefs, often to do with ideas about childhood, family and school are laid down when we are very young. The Map of Reality is reinforced by positive emotions and confirmed by beliefs added by others. It acts as a map because this conditioning leads us to repeat the same routes and take the same paths time and again.

Consider my childhood: I went to a private school and although I was rebellious in nature and ended up hating the rules, I was still conditioned by part of my schooling. Jim on the other hand, who regarded his time at school as very negative, was not so conditioned. I am explaining this so you can start to look at the person who judges you harshly as conditioned. They are probably not trying to sabotage or hurt you. Rather, they are trying to understand, but are coming up with conditioned responses to do with their Map of Reality.

If your friend or husband or parent is dead against you home educating, the best thing to do is allow them time to come round to the idea. They will see the smiles on the kids' faces as proof that they are happier. You can gently say factual things like, 'We concentrate more on tasks when we feel safe and secure, rather than scared or anxious', or 'Kids learn better when they don't even realise it's learning' and so on. Practice your strewing with them too! Strew some home-ed timetables for meet-ups and workshops and events; strew a book about learning or home education in the loo, just lying around for them to pick up.

Going head-to-head with somebody's deeply held beliefs about how the world works, or trying to pop their bubble before they are ready, will only breed resentment and negative critique. You do not need that. After all, if you have made this decision based on what is best for your kids, and it is working, then that is all you need to know.

Please do not look for validation for your efforts from someone who does not understand. Call that home educator parent you met at the group instead. Work on your own self-growth and self-esteem and soon everyone around you will not only see how you have made a change for the better, they will *feel* it too.

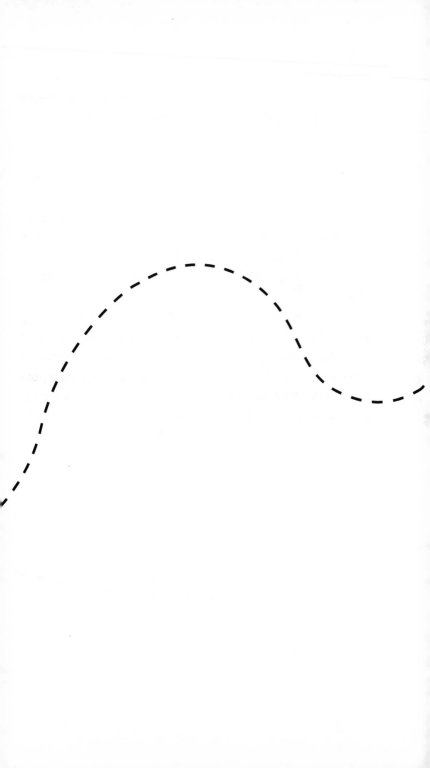

We don't need to reject or disparage technology. We need to put it in its place.

Sherry Turkle

Chapter 13
21st Century Kids

The question of 'screen time' is often the subject of debates among parents. It is important to debate this subject because that is how we develop insight into it. It is a relatively new subject too – not so long ago, this debate did not exist in the same way.

In the 1980s and 1990s, television was programmed very differently, with set shows at set times, available on a single screen in the corner of the living room. Since then, throughout the first two decades of the twenty-first century, it has evolved and developed dramatically in its pace, its content and how we experience it. For example, with on-demand services, we now have the ability to enjoy what we want, as and when we want to view it. For the first time, individuals are in charge of what they see and watch. Algorithms record and analyse what we choose to view and then they show us more, so it is harder to pull ourselves away from our own targeted stimulus. This is both incredibly freeing and confining.

But the big change since my childhood is the constant connectivity offered by the internet. I see the internet as a glorious tool for us, the common people of this beautiful planet to communicate freely together and learn from each other in a way that has never been available before. It is something to be admired and used in a way to benefit and awaken our possibilities.

How does this fit into home educating? Well, in my opinion, it can fit exceptionally nicely; if done with an objective and conscious mind-set. We have the power to source everything we need to create an amazing learning environment in our homes, from our homes. We can look up curriculums and find a vast array of subjects to study and learn about; we can communicate with others globally and create connections and possibilities as our kids grow.

However, we need to be aware of how we use new devices and maintain a conscious, mindful approach. As with any new tool, our use of the internet needs to be practiced and learnt carefully, and I feel we are still at a very excited, infantile time in our exploration of it. One of my convictions in life is that too much of anything prevents you becoming a balanced and grounded individual.

Device addiction

Screens – including electronic games and television – produce high definition distractions and do not foster consciousness. In fact, these systems are in place so readily for us precisely in order to distract and bombard us with advertising. This creates the opposite of consciousness, it creates a society in trance. An entranced society readily feels fear and wants to comfort itself with things. This is happening whether we choose to play a role in it or not, and it is not my place to try and stop it. I believe it will continue as long as people continue not to see it. I do feel however, it is my place to create consciousness and help people to wake up!

Devices like smartphones have been designed to produce instant gratification within us. Just like the slot machines in a casino, they are programmed to give us little and repeated hits of good-feeling dopamine, and on a neurological level they attempt to programme us to want more. This makes sense as a sales tactic and we should be ready to see much more of this in years to come with pheromones and sounds and colours to produce emotional attachment and a primal urge within us to need these things. This is marketing: as long as we are aware of it we are not so easily or readily programmed.

With screen time, social media and smartphones come a responsibility to ourselves. Like anything that gives instant gratification, their use must become a conscious thing and not a habitual programme you become a slave to. The word addiction comes from the Latin word *addictus*, which meant the assigning of a debtor to his/her creditor, or a slave to his/her master. That is food for thought, an addiction is not the master, but the arrangement between the substance and the addict.

I have seen many addictions in my therapy room, from food or cigarettes, to drugs and social media. To me, the substance is irrelevant. It always boils down to choice and responsibility to choose the best thing for ourself, and not to fill a void or create a crutch. When we are needlessly or unconsciously checking our phones or gaming for hours on end, or watching video after video on YouTube without a real focus or conscious desire, we are programming a habitual behaviour. We need to wake up and take responsibility for ourselves, and for our children, who are soaking up our behaviours all the time.

Ask yourself, 'Do I need this now? Do I want this now? Why do I want this?' This constant evaluation needs to become a habitual thing itself. Asking questions such as these will make your conscious self more aware of your behaviour and your emotional pulls. You are using the frontal lobe, the brain of logic and reason. By doing this, you will be showing your kids a way to achieve balance and happiness.

In his book about anxiety called *Clear Your Head*, Tim Box says that the big innovation in education will be when we start to teach people how to protect themselves from this constant bombardment of potentially negative information input. As home educators, we get to do this now, rather than wait for it to become part of a national curriculum! And I believe it all starts with this responsibility to show our children how to be mindful.

I feel that in times to come, we will settle down, and families will regain a balance of time together unplugged and time plugged in, but for now we need to begin this thought revolution. Home educators are revolutionary in many aspects of their life anyway. By taking control of our life rather than subjecting ourselves to state-run ideals, we are already choosing to be more conscious. So I am trusting in the fact that we can do this successfully with the internet also, to get the best out of this momentous and incredible experience at our fingertips, and to embrace the wonder and freedom it brings.

Finding balance

We are parents of children who have always had the internet, and yet most of us did not. It is bound to be difficult sometimes, but I suspect that our children will more easily and readily become masters of future communication than we will. The world is moving so quickly into an age of technology, and I do not want my children to be left behind. Yet at the same time, I want them to play in dirt and to be able to make a fire. This sort of reasoning is totally practical and healthy. This is how I balance my opinion when I have a mini-meltdown.

Mary Aiken's book *The Cyber Effect* unravels many stories and theories arising from behaviours online. It is worth a read to spark a debate within your own mind and draw attention to your own experience online. I stand by my point earlier, that it is our guidance and modelling of behaviour as parents that will ultimately pave the way for our children. If we retain a conscious effort of seeking balance and open communication together, everything will be OK.

It is wise to remember that there is no such thing as a perfect parent or a perfect life. Whatever we do, our kids will have issues with us and their environment and their childhood. That is just life. As home educators, we can have more of a say about how they grow up, but at the end of the day our kids will hold their own opinions. If we are coming from a conscious, aware and loving stance that is the best we can do.

In our household, the boys love to game. They play

online with other children and they play on separate consoles with each other and in groups. I have sat in and watched hours of this and seen various forms of strategizing, socialisation and responsibility play out between them. I have witnessed frustration, anger, restlessness and more unsavoury responses. I have also witnessed incredible kindness, competition, compassion, creativity, bravery and debates unfold that are sorted out between the kids themselves through times of emotional highs and lows.

I analyse my own conditioned thoughts, as a person who grew up without this as part of my life, and compare them against the reality I see happening and consciously try to ascertain a balanced opinion. In complete honesty, I go round in circles. We have had times with no consoles, when I have removed them; we have had set times off and on gaming; we have had go-with-the-flow, and to tell the truth, I am never satisfied. This says more about me than my children though. It is my own schooling that is dictating the message and I strive to be more conscious and less programmed by my conditioning.

I read somewhere that in the nineteenth century there was a debate whether to ban books, because when fiction started to become readily available people became so obsessed there was worry that they would lose part of their minds and not be able to function in the real world. This did make me giggle as part of my conditioned voice says this about gaming and that books are better somehow. See – different addictive substance, same programmed opinions and concerns!

There is a lot of hype around security and 'stranger

danger' online (and offline for that matter) but I do think it is partly scaremongering. Obviously, a code of conduct should be in place and discussed, but that just seems to be part of parenting, right? Being sensible with information and clued up to possible dangers should be part of educating our kids in life.

I wonder whether anxiety around this subject is greater because parents do not fully understand the internet, gaming, or online chatrooms. The answer to that is to properly educate yourself. It is the way the whole culture is going, from dating to job interviews, meetings and training, so to be left behind because of fear is a form of ignorance. If you do not participate in this area of society by choice, fair enough, but do not be surprised when your kids rebel against that.

Peeling kids off the screen

Sometimes I have to force my kids off their consoles. I know they have been gaming for too long and they are so absorbed in that other world they are almost in a trance state; time has melted away from them and they are unaware of life outside. This in itself is OK. To get lost in something you enjoy is no bad thing as long as you rebalance, so it is down to me as their guide to help them learn this – and yes sometimes I am seen as the bad guy!

I stay calm and consistent in my language and intent. I stand still and I speak slowly and quietly; there is absolutely no point in my emotions getting in the way as I will create a pattern in my household that no one wishes for. The kids get all blustery and huffy and I stand my ground quietly and resolutely. I give them a chance to debate their point, which is usually one more game, or five more minutes but I say no, and I repeat my intent. Each time, the time I have to wait gets shorter because they now know I will not back down.

It has taken practice and effort to achieve this. I have learned this approach from my job and my studies of emotional intelligence and behaviour, and I assure you it will work as long as you keep your own emotions in check. The moment you lose it, it is game over, and you are back at square one and in for the long haul again. So it is worth sticking with it.

It is a good plan to give the kids a warning about fifteen minutes before you expect them to come off the screens, and then a secondary warning two minutes before, as a reminder. Then before you go in, take some full and deep breaths and visualise what it is you plan to do once the kids are off the screens. Imagine you all going for a walk or popping out, whatever it is, and breathe it in. Then stand tall and stride in with a calm confidence but remain still and quiet in your manner. This will take practice especially if your kids have attached a fight to coming off the screens previously. It will take time but you have plenty of that!

After five minutes back in the real world, walking the dogs, playing outside or going somewhere, the kids will be focussed on reality and not the screens and you have achieved balance. When we have imbalance emotional issues can arise. If there are tantrums and adverse behaviour such as never wanting to leave the house, it can be easy to blame the substance (games or screens) rather than look at the wider picture. My advice is try and stay calm and not jump into a pre-conditioned programme of anger or emotion yourself. Try your hardest to see things objectively and see the whole picture. Ask yourself why you feel that way, and allow your mind to debate the answers.

At the end of the day, we are in charge of our household, not the children, and if you believe screens are damaging your kid's behaviour then do the right thing, detox. But I do suggest you look at your own behaviour, as well as that of adults around the children, to see the source of the learning and not just simply blame the screens!

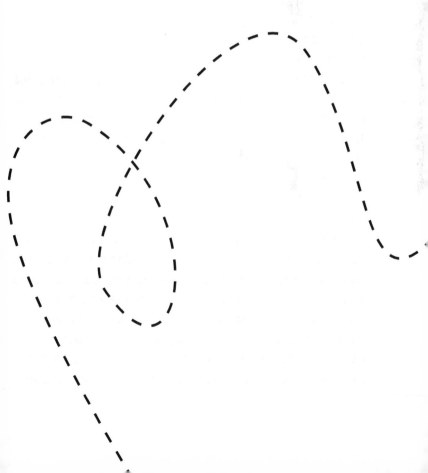

You are the bows from which your children as living arrows are sent forth.

Kahlil Gibran

Conclusion
Choose Your Own Adventure

To home educate is an act of consciousness, because to even entertain the idea you have to open your eyes and your heart to a different way of life. To make the choice and take the step into this other world.

As a nation and as a global community, we are waking up. I believe the internet has a lot to do with this new awareness. The fact we can easily communicate across society and culture has allowed a freedom of thought to gain momentum. We are creating a microcosm of openness and change, by resisting the conditioned belief that to learn is to be schooled. The opposite holds more truth. To be unschooled and curious is to find learning everywhere.

I am very excited at the prospect of individuals stepping up to the task of looking after and nurturing our children because it has a wider impact. When people take responsibility and don't pass the buck, a higher level of emotional intelligence is being developed. Home educators live in a state of higher emotional communication and are producing resilient and creative children who have self-respect and have harnessed confidence in themselves.

What this means for future generations is very exciting to someone like me, who is obsessed with bringing about self-empowerment and self-confidence in everybody everywhere. We are living in a time of transition and to see more people home educating each year is proof of this.

With the huge increase in people coming to home education, I hope the state will start to question how they are running the school system and implement changes more quickly than they seem to be at present. Looking to the future, I hope that home education becomes a choice for everyone, that it becomes so accessible through flexible working hours and equal partnerships in the home that everyone at least considers it as a choice, rather than having to find it the hard way – by being let down by the system.

Meanwhile, my family and many, many others will be getting on with our lives, learning all the time.

Welcome to a new age of thinking and the dawn of change!

Ideas for Further Reading

Mary Aiken, *The Cyber Effect*
This book from a leading cyberpsychologist offers a balanced argument for awareness around the online experience. Mary has helped me form my own view of the dangers of the internet, as well as how to use it as a tool to enhance our lives.

Clark Aldrich, *Unschooling Rules*
This book is an unschooling wonder. It is concise and to the point, and each short chapter rolls off the previous one to create a pathway to understanding. It is a great book to lend to curious or critical friends, and it has validated the unschool method in so many ways for us.

Steve Biddulph, *More Secrets to Happy Children*
This man has helped me so much as a parent. His writing about children is full of gentle appreciation, even when dealing with the big questions. Steve outlines family

balance and emotional understanding, and offers ways to achieve them in your own life.

Tim Box, *Clear Your Head*

Remedial hypnotist and anxiety expert Tim outlines the system of change that I use in my therapy work with clients. This book's easy to read, conversational style gives insight and knowledge into anxiety, why we all need it in our lives and how to get CONTROL of it.

Joe Dispenza, *Becoming Supernatural*

'Dr. Joe' is fast becoming a guru of energy healing. He explains so many huge topics like neuroscience, quantum physics and emotional intelligence and yet makes them understandable and logical. This book shows how each of us has limitless possibility to become the best version of ourselves.

Sandra Dodd, *Big Book of Unschooling*

This is the book to read on how to Unschool. Sandra's unforgiving voice of reason is what I needed to shake me up, and decide what I wanted for my life. This book has a wealth of topic ideas and ways to incorporate learning into everyday living, which is the beating heart of unschooling.

Emma Gannon, *The Multi-Hyphen Method*

This book is a fabulous read for anyone who wants a flexible working life and multiple income streams. Emma predicts how, in the future, everyone will be working more efficiently and flexibly, giving a work-life balance that the majority have not yet even dreamt of.

John Taylor Gatto, *Weapons of Mass Instruction* and *Dumbing Us Down*
Esteemed educator Gatto describes the political undercurrents of the school system. He explains why and how education is dumbing us down, based on his first-hand experience as a teacher. He was an activist for his vision that every child should have their own unique curriculum to work from, created by the individual.

Kahil Gibran, *The Prophet*
Poet, philosopher and artist Gibran tells the story of the prophet, and as he does so, he explains poetically and insightfully about many of life's experiences, such as love, marriage and children.

John Holt, *Learning All the Time* and *How Children Fail*
Unschooling pioneer and the daddy of home educating. John stood up for the homeschool method in the early years and was a great help to many. His books are full of reasoning as to why home education is the way forward, and why children benefit so much from this approach.

Maxwell Maltz, *Psycho-Cybernetics*
This book is an epic insight into how the mind works. Maltz's explanation of the human brain as a creative mechanism is intriguing. He includes many first-hand stories, and encourages the reader to use the book as a course in self discovery and betterment.

Daniel J. Siegel and Tina Payne Bryson, *The Whole-brain Child Workbook: Practical Exercises, Worksheets*

and Activities to Nurture Developing Minds
Dr Siegel is a neuropsychiatrist and parenting expert. He
is a master of emotional intelligence. Every parent should
get this workbook; it is so helpful when dealing with
crises, our own emotional conflicts and conditioning.

Online Resources
***The Ultimate History Lesson: A Weekend with John
Taylor Gatto*** (directed by Richard Andrew Grove, 2012)
Search the John Taylor Gatto TV channel on YouTube.

And two essential websites that collate information and
resources about home education and the law in the UK.
They contain a wealth of knowledge:

Educational Freedom www.educationalfreedom.org.uk
Education Otherwise www.educationotherwise.org

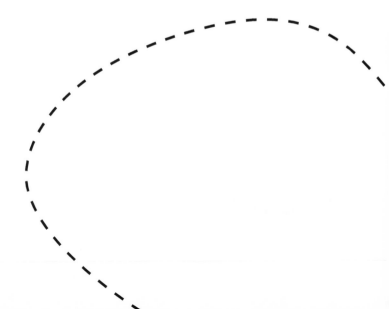

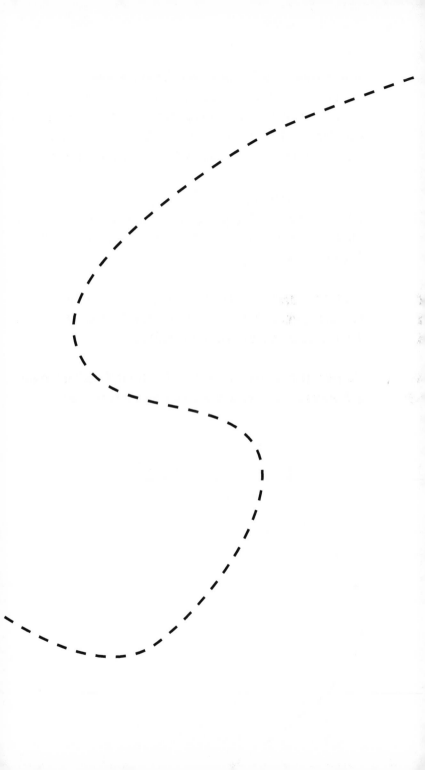

Made in the USA
Monee, IL
18 January 2020